DR. JEB S. HU

TEAM RELATIONSHIP MANAGEMENT

THE ART OF CRAFTING EXTRAORDINARY TEAMS

Printed and bound in the United States of America

Cover Design ©2019 by Elena A. Newton
Interior Design and Editing by: Elena A. Newton

Many thanks to the developers at Affinity Serif Publisher® for building the greatest publishing software in the universe. ~ean

ISBN 978-0-578-51880-0
First Edition First Printing

Library of Congress Control Number:
2019905964

Published by:
Xmetryx Press
an Imprint of Xmetryx, LLC
Scottsdale, AZ USA
www.xmetryx.com
press@xmetryx.com

Hey cuz!
Can't wait to hear your thoughts on this :)
Thank you for supporting us!!
:) Elena

In memory of my Dad

I found inspiration and purpose through my memories of his habit of trying to see the potential in people; his love of teaching and mentoring; his curiosity about people and their stories; and his seeing success in terms of the richness of relationships.

Bill,
Thank you for your support!
All the best!

Acknowledgements

This book would never have come together without the encouragement, patience, and perseverance of my Xmetryx Co-Founder, editor, muse, best friend, and life partner. Thank you, Elena. You are amazing!

And a sincere thank you to the many people on my teams at HP, and my friends in Singapore and around the world who provided feedback and input to my ideas and articles during the two-plus years this work was in progress. Last, a very big and heartfelt thank you to the group of talented people who were willing to endure a rough manuscript and provide invaluable feedback: Pam Newton, Gido van Praag, Dennis Pitocco, Meredith Savadove, Sidi Wang, and my daughter, Devan. Your inspiring words and suggestions helped to bring these ideas to life.

Table of Contents

Introduction

"There's a way to do it better–find it."

~Thomas Edison

Every person, place, or idea has a story. This one started seven years ago when I began a quest to answer, for myself, three questions that I regularly asked the people I mentored and coached:

> Where do you find the most meaning and purpose in your work?
>
> How will you stay relevant in the face of continuous change?
>
> How can you make a difference that matters to more than just an audience of one: what will be your "small dent in the universe?" to quote the late Steve Jobs.

My answer to the first question emerged as I uncovered the themes that formed the narrative of my 30+ year career: my passion for coaching and mentoring; a deep curiosity about why people do what they do (which has always been my source of energy for innovation and challenging the status quo); and my drive to create and build, versus maintain and manage. I found the answer to the third question in the joy of helping people through one of their most significant career transitions—moving from individual contributor to people manager.

Answering the second question was the toughest because I had to set aside the ego and identity that comes with "I was CEO of this" and "I was a vice-president of that," and see my career experiences for what they really were—a history on which I could build, not laurels on which I should rest. That shift in mindset gave me the courage and conviction to invest in a five-year 'walkabout' in the shoes of today's team leaders, rather than returning to a senior leadership role. I also recognized that walking in those other shoes would only be truly valuable if I complemented that experience with a deeper understanding of contemporary team leadership. So, I took a deep-dive into the fields of human motivation, employee engagement, and team effectiveness, earning a doctorate in the process.

The idea of Team Relationship Management (TRM) was built upon the shoulders of giants. It reflects the voices of the thousands of employees I encountered through research studies and both formal and informal conversations; my doctoral research and the many scholars that contributed to my work; and direct conversations with hundreds of team leaders. It also echoes the voice of my late father, a history teacher turned businessman. As he made the transition from academia to business, he never lost his love of teaching and mentoring, or his insatiable curiosity about people and the stories they shared with him. Most significantly, he saw success in terms of the strength of the relationships that he developed with both employees and customers.

What emerged from those many voices became the architecture of TRM:

- The essential fundamentals of team relationships
- The core psychological needs that inspire individual motivation
- The relationship coaching practices that lead to strong, trusting relationships

The overarching theme within TRM is powerful yet simple: people want and need healthy relationships at work to do their best and be their best. So human. So blindingly obvious. While there are mountains of research that demonstrate the importance people dynamics has on team effectiveness and individual well-being, the concept of actively managing relationships is largely absent from the vocabulary and metrics of business leaders. Nor will you find it in the training programs and models used by most leader development consultancies and leadership gurus such as Tuckman's 1965 Forming-Storming-Norming-Performing; the GRPI model (goals-roles-processes-interpersonal relationship, 1977); the T7 model, or Katzenbach and Smith's Commitment-Skills-Accountability in the 1990's; or the Five Dynamics and The Hackman Model from the early 2000's. All these models contain useful ideas, but they all reflect the 20th-century bias toward top-down, leader-centric hierarchies.

Interest in the relationship dimension of teams isn't entirely missing from modern organizations, and it has garnered more attention in the early 21st century than most of the 20th century. Yet, too often, relationships are treated as a secondary aspect in teamwork models, or as an outcome of climbing ropes together or building tinker toy objects while blindfolded. The stellar exceptions can be found among teams such as the US Navy SEALs. In his excellent book *Team of Teams,* General Stanley McChrystal (U.S. Army, retired), the former commander of the Joint Special Operations Task Force in Iraq and Afghanistan, paints a vivid picture of the essence of crafting extraordinary teams as he describes the ambition of the Navy SEAL basic training. McChrystal emphasizes that the training's goal is "not to produce supersoldiers. It is to build superteams."

Amazingly—despite the overwhelming evidence that fostering strong, trusting relationships is the foundation of every high-performance team—most organizations do little or nothing to train leaders to actively manage the key relationships that make or break team effectiveness and well-being. As CRM did for sales effectiveness in the 20th century, TRM offers what may be the single most significant opportunity for organizations to ensure that their teams can innovate and compete in the 21st century. Moreover, as people transition from individual contributor to people manager, establishing habits that lead to excellence can make or break both careers and organizations. Making TRM a cornerstone of that transition ensures that your teams have the energy, adaptability, and resilience to excel.

This book is a practical guide for a new generation of team leaders. Whether you're taking on your first people leadership role in a large company, or leading a fast-growing start-up, you are as passionate about people's welfare as you are about performance. You recognize the importance of your role to your organization; yet, too often, you don't get the support you need to complement your hands-on experience with ideas and tools to put your team on the road to extraordinary. In a nod to my brother's input and his enlightened approach to leadership, the concepts in this book will also prove useful to senior business leaders who want to stay relevant in the 21st century. This book is for those of you who understand that 20th-century approaches aren't good enough for today's challenges and are looking for new ideas to spur innovation, attract and retain talent, and develop the next generation of leaders.

I recognize that there are many dimensions of successfully leading and developing a team (i.e., getting the right people, establishing goals, designating roles, establishing processes). They are well covered in many books and articles on leadership, as well as in my previous book, *The ONE Habit,* so I won't revisit them here. Instead, I offer a new and innovative perspective centered around relationships. Over the course of my research, I discovered that, along with the practices associated with leading any team, managing relationships holds the key to crafting an extraordinary team.

As a team leader, or any leader for that matter, your days often feel like you're changing tires on a moving car. I did my best to write this book with that in mind. If you're reading this introduction in anticipation of what's to come, I ask you to occasionally indulge my passion for business history. Beyond that, you won't get a lot of pop-psychology buzz words and business speak clichés. You'll also be disappointed if you're looking for a list of 15 ways to improve performance. Rather, in five parts I'll take you from the rise of teams in the 20th century to three specific actions that, no matter how crazy busy you are, you can take immediately to begin developing the habits that lead to mastering the art of crafting an extraordinary team.

Part 1. The Rise of Teams looks back at the twentieth-century world of Frederick Taylor's Scientific Management and the 'hierarchy-and-heroes' approach to leadership, then traces the evolution of teams into the 21st century. I discuss how success in the 21st century demands that organizations reshape themselves around teams and networks of teams, and what it takes to enable a new generation of team leaders to thrive.

Part 2. Want Extraordinary? Get Relationships. examines the chemistry of exceptional teams and what it will take to ensure that your team is ready for the demands of the 21st century. Today's teams are responsible for increasingly complex tasks, and play an ever greater role in delivering both longer-term innovation and immediate results. Whether working locally or virtually across time zones and cultures, they must demonstrate an unprecedented level of adaptability. We'll look at the relationship between balancing performance with well-being, and the importance of embracing the idea that success depends less on a leader's skills or brilliance, and more on their humility and ability to inspire the best in people.

Part 3. Team Relationship Management begins with an examination of the tension between the drive for productivity and efficiency, and the needs of employees, that defined management thinking throughout the 20th century. We'll then turn to the late 20th and early 21st century developments in understanding human motivation, employee engagement, and team effectiveness that led to the development of Team Relationship Management. Last, we'll define and explore each of the elements of the TRM architecture in detail:

- The team relationship fundamentals that are critical to establishing a highly-functional team culture.
- The core psychological needs that, when met, inspire individual motivation and energize people to do their best work.
- Team relationship coaching: the core leadership practice that drives effectiveness and well-being.

Part 4. The Core of TRM: Coaching Your Team gives you the nuts and bolts of the one habit shared by every exceptional team leader: relationship coaching. The chapter starts by answering the question: Why relationship coaching? We'll reflect on personal coaching conversation philosophies, and the differences in mindsets and behavior that lead to highly effective coaching. The chapter then dives into the specifics of feedback, measuring and tracking the strength of team relationships, followed by relationship coaching strategies, improving your coaching conversations, and how to plan for those conversations. We'll wrap-up discussing how TRM is designed to be an integral part of modern continuous performance management programs.

Part 5. Crafting an Extraordinary Team asks you to reflect on two questions: "Why does my team want to be led by me?" and, "Am I creating the best conditions for my team to thrive in terms of both performance and well-being?" I'll help you to answer those questions by building upon the groundwork established in the prior chapters and summarizing the three actions that you can take immediately to put you and your team on the road to extraordinary.

Throughout the book, you'll find pages for notes, a glossary, and select references. In the appendices, you'll find information on Xmetryx TRM™ software tools for team leaders, as well as my TRM Workshop™ and, in Appendix C, a deep-dive into the behavioral science research foundation of Team Relationship Management.

As this book came together, there was discussion around printing a hardcover version, or only softcovers. I resisted the temptation for hardcover because people often don't like to write in a hard-bound book. My hope is that the ideas in this book are sufficiently compelling that you are inspired to make notes, dog-ear pages, and (most importantly) embrace the concepts, making them part of your own approach to crafting an extraordinary team.

Connect with me on LinkedIn and let me know how you're doing crafting your extraordinary team. Good reading!

Jeb

The Rise of Teams

"History doesn't repeat itself, but it does rhyme."

–Mark Twain

In the 20th century, business news was dominated by tales of hero bosses single-handedly transforming their organizations through command and control of the legions beneath them. Celebrity CEOs in the later part of the century—from Lee Iacocca of Chrysler, to Stanley Gault of Rubbermaid, and 'Chainsaw' Al Dunlap of Sunbeam—placed as much (or more) emphasis on PR, gracing the cover of Business Week, and ghost-written biographies as they did on performance. Teams, while increasingly important, typically resided in organizational silos and were charged with implementing plans handed down from above as efficiently and cost-effectively as possible. This 'hierarchy-and-heroes' model of managing large organizations had its roots in the revolution put in motion by Frederick Winslow Taylor at the 1900 Paris Exposition Universelle.

Taylor, the son of a Princeton-educated lawyer and raised as a Quaker outside of Philadelphia, opted to leave his appointed path that was to take him from a prestigious prep school to Harvard, and become an apprentice patternmaker and machinist at the Enterprise Hydraulic Works in Philadelphia, PA. Upon completing his apprenticeship, he became a machine-shop laborer at the Midvale Steel Works. Taylor's experience working on the shop floor drove his passion for improving process efficiency. Taylor, who wrote that "the best management is a true science, resting upon clearly defined laws, rules, and principles," summed up his efficiency techniques in the 1911 book *The Principles of Scientific Management*, and subsequently made his fortune from steel process-improvement patents. Prior to the emergence of his 'Scientific Management' method, ascension into management was largely considered a reward for years of service, resulting in higher pay and less physical work. Under Taylor's new system, managers were charged with the thinking and planning, while workers executed tasks that were broken down into their simplest elements. By the early part of the 20th century, entrepreneurs such as Henry Ford and Andrew Carnegie were applying the tenets of scientific management and hyper-specialization in their factories, dramatically improving efficiency and profits.

The two World Wars accentuated the importance of efficiency—especially in manufacturing and supply chains—and demonstrated the critical need for creativity and continuous innovation that was most likely to come from smaller, focused groups. During and after WWII, the US military played a crucial role in recognizing the need to add fast and flexible 'special forces' capabilities to the operations of large standing armies. Building upon the example of British Commandos, the U.S. military formed the Marine Raiders, Army Rangers, and the

Pacific Underwater Demolition Teams—the foundation of today's Navy SEALs. While Taylor's view that efficiency was central to organizational success continued to influence organizations through the end of the 20th century, by the 1980s most large organizations were committed to creating their own special forces in the form of more autonomous business units. At the same time, within engineering and software development departments a more organic and people-centric approach to accelerate the innovation-to-market cycle was in its genesis: agile software development.

Jim Highsmith and Alistair Cockburn, two founders of the agile development process and authors of the Agile Manifesto, understood that—in order to thrive in the face of increasing complexity and accelerating change—organizations needed to become more adaptive and people-centric. They argued that [development] teams would benefit from decentralization and collaboration, with simple guidelines that would encourage finding creative ways to solve problems as they arose. This agile approach was a stark contrast to scientific management's all-encompassing, hyper-detailed rules that depended on describing the practices and conditions for every situation in advance. Agile processes, by contrast, were designed to capitalize on everyone's unique strengths, with processes being selected, tailored, and adapted to the people on a project team.

As we move toward the end of the second decade of the 21st century, the technology-fueled, globalized business world is driving a level of complexity, speed of change, and degree of networked interdependence that is unprecedented. Few leaders today believe that the lifeblood of their organization is efficiency, nor do they believe that the siloed, hierarchy-and-heroes approach of the 20th century is the path to 21st-century success. While efficiency remains an essential part of most companies' strategy, it is the ability to adapt to complexity, and demonstrate resilience in the face of continual change, that has become the imperative.

Thriving in the 21st century demands that organizations reshape themselves around teams and networks of teams, and that senior leaders transform people's mindsets from leadership belonging to a single person or specific role, to leadership as a collaborative process that is shared across networks of people. Most senior leaders embrace the idea that teams determine whether their organization ends up as a historical footnote, languishes in mediocrity, or is on the road to enduring greatness. The challenge is driving the transformations within their organizations that enable a new generation of leaders to thrive.

Chapter Highlights

- The 20th century was dominated by a 'hierarchy-and-heroes' narrative of bosses who were portrayed as transforming their organizations through command and control of the legions beneath them.
- Teams, while increasingly important, typically resided in organizational silos and were charged with implementing plans handed down from above.
- Top-down hierarchy had its roots in Taylor's scientific management. Managers were charged with planning and efficiency, while workers executed highly-detailed tasks.
- The two World Wars accentuated the importance of efficiency, but also demonstrated the need for creativity and continuous innovation that more often came from smaller groups of 'special forces'.
- By the 1980s, most large organizations were committed to creating their own special forces in the form of more autonomous business units.

- With the advent of agile development, simple guidelines encouraged finding creative ways to solve problems as they arose—a stark contrast to scientific management's all-encompassing, hyper-detailed rules.
- Today's organizations must reshape themselves around teams and networks of teams and transform people's mindsets from leadership being a person, to leadership as a collaborative, shared process.

Thoughts & Notes

What trends are affecting you and your team?

How are you reshaping your team's mindset from leadership being a person, to leadership as a shared process?

Thoughts & Notes

Want Extraordinary? Get Relationships.

"The world is moving so fast these days that the man who says it can't be done is generally interrupted by someone doing it."

~Elbert Hubbard

Extraordinary teams have a chemistry that enables them to consistently deliver exceptional results. This chemistry is neither a matter of luck nor an accident of evolution—it's a product of single-minded preparation and a steadfast determination to excel. These teams focus on developing the few habits that lead to excellence: laying a foundation of enduring trust, encouraging behaviors that inspire, and coaching that keeps relationships healthy. Most impressively, extraordinary teams combine adaptability, resilience, and a relentless will to win with a collective selflessness.

In *Team of Teams,* General McChrystal emphasizes that "The formation of a SEAL team is less about preparing people to follow precise orders than it is about developing trust and the ability to adapt within a small group." Despite the critical role that teams play in an organization's success, few companies take lessons from the SEAL playbook and ensure that, from day one, new leaders develop the skills and habits required to forge an adaptable and resilient unit that consistently delivers superior performance. Just like the SEALs, the key is to make early development experiences meaningful and formative by coaching new leaders to embrace a mindset that focuses on inspiring the energy, motivation, and engagement of their people.

Ensuring that your team is ready for the demands of the 21st century means being capable of planning, problem-solving, and decision making as an integrated unit. Creating the chemistry that is the catalyst for excellence will test your ability to work locally and virtually across both time zones and cultural boundaries, uniting people across borders while acknowledging their individuality. You must learn to motivate, communicate, and collaborate through a combination of shared leadership practices and digital technologies, seeing shared leadership and collaboration as essential to building highly-effective teams.

Many of the examples of exceptional teams (including my own) come from the military, surgical units, firefighters, sports, or (less frequently) the corporate world. They tend to be easy to spot because what they do, along with their impact, is so visible. However, one of the great pleasures I've experienced in researching and writing this book is that when I looked a little harder, I found extraordinary teams in many places. In one example, over the course of four years, I had a front-row seat watching a team come together to turn an unremarkable hotel bar into a 'must visit' destination nightspot, ranked number one in Asia and number three in the world.

My first visit to Manhattan at the Regent Hotel in Singapore was in 2014 on the recommendation of a coworker who found it to be a 'nice, quiet spot' for a post-work get-together or catching up with friends. What was most memorable from that first visit was my conversation with Manhattan's new General Manager, Philip Bischoff, who had recently arrived in Singapore from Berlin. We chatted about his ambitions to create a truly remarkable experience on every dimension, from the ambiance to the craft-cocktails and personalized service. It all sounded great—and a lot like the mission statements of many other leaders. However, when I asked him how he was going to accomplish that very ambitious goal in the notoriously challenging Singapore Food and Beverage (F&B) environment, his answer was anything but typical: "I'm not going to do it. I'm going to bring together a group of people who will."

Philip's tenure at Manhattan coincided with my doctoral research, and the overlap in our respective ambitions made for an excellent informal case study. What unfolded was a stunning example of crafting an extraordinary team from the ground up. From day one, Philip laid a foundation that set the stage for excellence. First, he communicated a clear, compelling purpose that included his ambition for Manhattan as well as why people would thrive there, and in parallel established a set of team values (norms) which included:

- Everyone owns the experience of every guest
- Everyone on the team has an equal voice
- Leadership is a team sport: everyone must play their position exceptionally well, and be ready to support or cover for a teammate at any time

Philip began investing in the development of people's skills across every role—giving people an opportunity to rotate through different positions, and travel to industry events and competitions. Very quickly, working at Manhattan became one of the most sought-after positions in the Singapore F&B industry. When I spoke with the people on the team, it was evident that everyone sharing the same goals, and Philip's investment in them was having a significant impact on their energy and confidence.

By year two, my conversations with team members began to take on a new tone. The chemistry and energy of the team was flowing over to guests, business was rapidly increasing, and the name Manhattan was beginning to catch the attention of industry watchers within Singapore and the Asia region. That same year, they were recognized as one of the Top 50 Bars in Asia. At this point, many leaders and their people declare victory and happily settle among the many 'above average' establishments. Yet, instead of resting on their well-earned laurels, the team collectively raised the bar with a goal of joining the list of Top Ten bars in Asia. In response, Philip doubled-down on people development and coaching. The results were nothing short of amazing. In 2016, just two years after opening, Manhattan took the number five spot in Asia. In both 2017 and 2018 they were recognized as #1 in Asia, and in 2018 over 500 experts in 58 countries recognized Manhattan as #3 in the world.

At the end of 2018, Philip was promoted to a senior role within the Four Season's organization. When we chatted at his farewell celebration, I asked him what he felt was the key to the extraordinary results. Without hesitation he said, "the team and their relationships—both with each other and with our guests."

Crafting an extraordinary team means embracing the idea that success in your role depends less on your skills or brilliance, and more on your humility and ability to inspire the best in people. It is essential that you live the ideal that only the group performs, and individuals contribute to this performance. If you've mastered the art of crafting an extraordinary team, then you get relationships.

Chapter Highlights

- The chemistry of exceptional teams is a product of single-minded preparation and a steadfast determination to excel. These teams focus on developing the few habits that lead to excellence:
    - Laying a foundation of enduring trust
    - Encouraging behaviors that inspire
    - Coaching that keeps relationships strong
- Extraordinary teams combine adaptability, resilience, and a relentless will to win with a collective selflessness.
- Learn to inspire the energy and engagement of your people by communicating and collaborating through a combination of shared leadership practices and digital technologies.
- Your role depends less on your skills or brilliance, and more on your humility and ability to inspire the best in people.
- Mastering the art of crafting an extraordinary team means learning to manage relationships.

Thoughts & Notes

How are you:

1. Laying a foundation of enduring trust?
2. Encouraging behaviors that inspire?
3. Coaching to keep relationships strong?

Thoughts & Notes

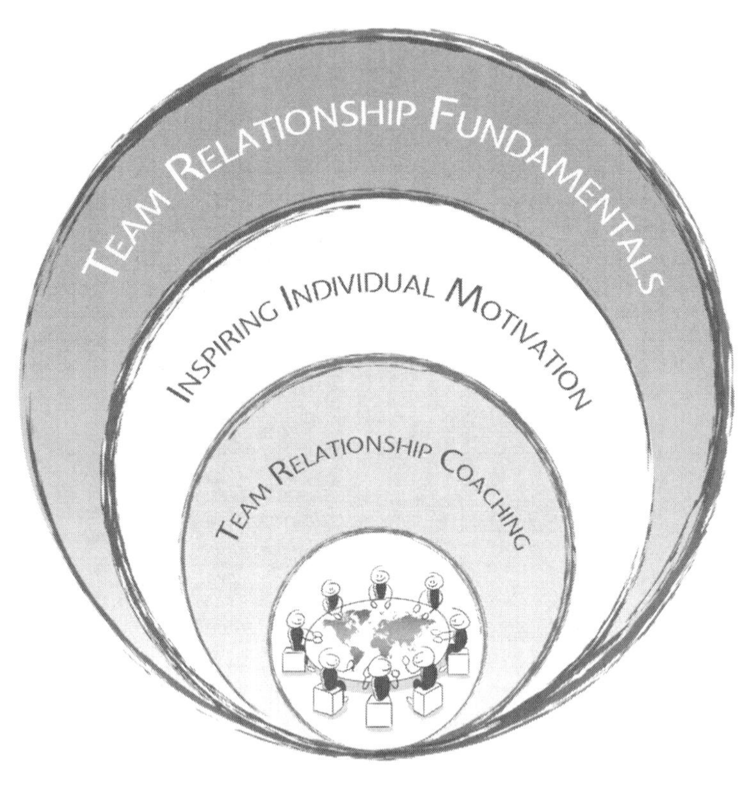

The Elements of the TRM Architecture

Team Relationship Management

"In the midst of chaos, there is also opportunity"

~Sun Tzu

The Relationship Architecture

While Taylor's star has been nearly extinguished, his ideas were a catalyst for the complementary human relations movement that laid much of the groundwork for contemporary approaches to teamwork in organizations. His ethos of planned efficiency dominated the worldview of business leaders, consultants, and academics for several generations. So long as change was essentially linear—tasks moving from one worker and department to another, and decision-making flowing up and down the organizational hierarchy—scientific management and its reductionist principles enabled companies to scale in a predictable fashion. However, the human cost of reducing tasks to their lowest common denominator was high.

The human relations movement began in the 1920s as a quest for balance between the "things of production" and the "humanity of production," terms coined by the Englishman Oliver Sheldon in 1923. Through the mid-20th century, people like Abraham Maslow (Maslow's Hierarchy of Needs) and MIT professor Douglas McGregor (Theory X and Theory Y) began advocating approaches to human relationship management that focused on the benefit of giving people the autonomy to motivate and control themselves. Building upon research done earlier in the century, professors Edward Deci and Richard Ryan published their work on self-determination theory (SDT) in the mid-1980s. Within SDT, Deci and Ryan describe the conditions under which people may achieve their potential and optimize their development, performance, and well-being. That tension between the drive for productivity and efficiency, and human needs, defined management thinking throughout the 20th century.

Over the past 30+ years, information technology revolutionized how businesses are created, compete, and grow. In parallel, SDT researchers have consistently shown that engaged, motivated individuals experience improved physical and psychological well-being. The highly-dynamic, and at times chaotic, nature of teamwork in a complex global—and often virtual—environment requires tremendous adaptability and resiliency. A better understanding of the fluid and complex nature of teamwork in flatter, networked organizations demands a greater emphasis on the people dynamics. To cultivate a highly-effective, adaptable, and resilient team, you must understand what motivates each person and develop the relationship management skills that foster trust, energy, and engagement.

Team Relationship Management (TRM) is an approach to improving the performance of your team, along with the well-being of the individuals on it, by developing strong, trusting relationships. The TRM concept originated at the intersection of research into human motivation, employee engagement, and team effectiveness. At the core of TRM is the dynamic of people's experiences versus their expectations. The power of TRM comes from identifying and measuring experience-expectation gaps and tracking relationship strength. Decades of research shows that disparities between people's experiences and expectations can harm relationships and diminish performance. Consistently addressing and closing relationship gaps builds the trust that spurs engagement, performance, and satisfaction. The design of the TRM architecture has three elements:

1. **Team Relationship Fundamentals:** establishing the clarity of purpose and healthy norms that are critical to a highly-functional culture.
2. **Inspiring Individual Motivation**: understanding the psychological needs that, when met, inspire and energize people to do their best for themselves and the team.
3. **Team Relationship Coaching**: the core leadership practice that drives team effectiveness and well-being.

In its essence, TRM is a set of practices that offer what may be the single most significant opportunity for organizations to ensure that their teams are able to innovate and compete in the 21st century. The rest of this chapter describes each element of the TRM architecture in more detail.

Element 1: Team Relationship Fundamentals

"Teamwork is the ability to work together toward a common vision, the ability to direct individual accomplishments toward organizational objectives. It is the fuel that allows common people to attain uncommon results.." ~Andrew Carnegie

---

What does it take to build and sustain an extraordinary team? In addition to discipline, patience, and perseverance, it starts with laying a foundation of strong team relationship fundamentals: a clear, compelling purpose and healthy norms.

A Clear and Compelling Purpose

It seems like such a no-brainer that a team should understand why it exists—and most do, up to a point. In my TRM workshop, the first group-exercise is to answer the question: "Why does your team exist?" Seems obvious, right? There are always a few eye rolls and 'this will be a waste of time' expressions. But, the devil is in the details. A click of the remote reveals the rules...Write a 2-3 sentence statement which considers the reason your team exists in terms of your:

- Value proposition to the broader organization
- Value proposition to customers/stakeholders
- Value proposition to team members

I've done this with many new first-level leaders as well as seasoned VP/GM's and Directors who wanted to experience the program that they were investing in for their people. Everyone quickly answers the first two questions (though the replies often sound like corporate mission statement), then virtually everyone gets stuck on the third one. The most common response is, "no one ever asked me that before." With a little guidance, and by framing the third value proposition with the example of recruiting a much-desired candidate, most of the leaders connect the dots. Purpose is about people. As a leader, a big part of your role is to make your team attractive to high-energy, talented people. You do that by being able to describe your team in terms of all three value propositions. You must also ensure that the job design of each member of your team is consistent with the reason for why your team exists (see the **Connecting Motivation and Job Design** sidebar).

In 2017, Claudine Gartenberg, Assistant Professor of Management at the Wharton School of the University of Pennsylvania, and her colleagues published the results of a large-scale study they conducted on Corporate Purpose and Financial Performance. They found that:

- An organization's purpose is not characterized by a formal announcement, but instead by a set of collective beliefs that are held by, and guide, the actions of employees.
- Companies with a strong purpose are characterized by employees that, in aggregate, have a strong sense of the meaningfulness and collective impact of their work.
- Organizations that demonstrate clarity of purpose among their knowledge workers, first-level leaders, and middle managers also exhibit superior accounting and stock market performance.

Developing a clear and compelling team purpose can be done in a relatively short amount of time by working through the following steps:

1. Develop a set of specific objectives and key results that align with the broader unit or organization goals.
2. Identify the key relationships, as well as the formal and informal communications processes, necessary to accomplish the goals of the team.
3. Describe the context in which the team will operate. For example, a global virtual, a co-located, or a permanent functional team.
4. List the key competencies people must have to be successful in delivering the team goals. Identify any gaps/areas to strengthen.
5. Reflecting on the goals, relationships, context, and competencies from the first four steps, develop a two- to three-sentence team purpose statement. Make sure it's clear and compelling.

Healthy Team Norms

Norms are the traditions, behavioral standards, and rules of your group that form your team's culture. They

Connecting Motivation and Job Design

Job design is related to the specification of contents, methods and relationship of jobs in a manner that meets both organizational and individual needs. Richard Hackman and Greg Oldham's job characteristics theory forms the foundation of many job design practices. The theory is based on the principle that employees derive motivation from completing a task. They suggest that high levels of motivation occur as a result of three critical psychological states:

- **Meaningfulness**: People must consider the task to be meaningful.
- **Responsibility**: People should have enough discretion to plan and carry out the task as they see fit.
- **Feedback**: People need to be aware of how effective they have been.

In turn, these psychological states were proposed to enhance employees' intrinsic motivation, job satisfaction, quality of work and performance, while reducing turnover.

Good job design should maximize people's energy and engagement in their work. In describing the purpose of any role, consider both the content and context. Role content includes goals, responsibilities, and competencies. Key dimensions of content include:

reflect the translation of individual values (e.g., respect for others') to collective expectations (we will be respectful of each person's right to speak). Be purposeful to incorporate values which set clear expectations for demonstrating emotional/social intelligence, psychological safety, and conversation equality. Here are a few examples of norms that came up in my conversations with team leaders:

- Honesty and candor from everyone
- We will work to see and eliminate bias
- Everyone is responsible for ensuring psychological safety and equality around the table
- We will deal with conflict quickly, fairly, and transparently

Most importantly, norms should be used to both guide and assess team behavior. Developing a healthy team culture is the most essential fundamental to get right.

Google and Project Aristotle

As one of the world's most visible companies, with a corporate motto of "Don't be Evil", the bar is high for Google in terms of team culture. In his article "What

Skill variety: The range of skills and activities necessary to complete the job. The greater the range of skills a person uses, the more motivating the work.

Task identity: The degree to which a job is holistic. People are more satisfied when they are involved in an activity from start to finish.

Task significance (purpose): This looks at the impact and influence of a job. Jobs are more satisfying if people believe that they are adding real value to colleagues, the organization, or the larger community.

Autonomy: This is the degree of individual choice involved in a job. More autonomy, and decision-making involvement, leads to more satisfaction.

Feedback: This is the amount of information a person receives about his or her performance, and the extent to which he or she can see the impact of the work.

Developing or crafting role content collaboratively with each team member can help ensure that they find meaning in the role and that it keeps them energized.

Role context includes clearly articulated team values, the important relationships upon which success depends, and how feedback is regularly gathered and communicated. This last element of job design, continual feedback, is critical to sustaining engagement as it ensures people know the results of their work.

Google Learned from Its Quest to Build the Perfect Team", Pulitzer Prize-winning reporter Charles Duhigg captured Google's passion for excellence and the critical role of norms. As described by Duhigg, at Google, the world revolves around data analytics and patterns, and this includes data about people. People analytics—data analysis focused on the patterns of peoples' behaviors and aimed at enhancing individual productivity—has been at the forefront of human resources development for more than a decade. This focus on individual performance has been beneficial. However, there is little in the way of people analytics that shows what consistently drives superior team performance. This gap between understanding individual productivity versus team effectiveness led Google's People Operations and People Analytics unit on a multi-year journey to uncover the drivers and differentiators of their most effective teams.

Code-named 'Project Aristotle', the researchers conducted a review of studies spanning 50-years, along with surveys and in-depth interviews with 180 teams within Google. Initially, the Aristotle team did not see an explanation for differences in team effectiveness. The first breakthrough came when the researchers began to look at the data through the lens of behavioral science theories on group values and people's experiences across key relationships. This new perspective created a crucial turning point for the Aristotle team. The results demonstrated the critical importance that values have on performance; however, it did not reveal any consistent patterns as to which values were shared by the most successful teams.

The second breakthrough came as the Aristotle team listened to their colleagues describe the experiences they were having on their teams, identified the patterns, and looked for correlations and causality with performance. The results identified "psychological safety" as the essential ingredient in the mix of norms that enabled a team to realize their potential. Psychological Safety, as described by Harvard Business School professor Amy Edmondson, is a "shared belief held by members of a team that the team is safe for interpersonal risk-taking, and a sense of confidence that the team will not embarrass, reject, or punish someone for speaking up." Most significantly, psychological safety describes an aspect of team culture where people feel they can trust others and be themselves.

With the "aha" of psychological safety in hand, the Project Aristotle team turned its attention to making the experience-based conversations—which lead to greater psychological safety and healthy norms—a habit for everyone at Google.

Exceptional teams are characterized by the health of key relationships, with norms such as listening and respect at the top of the values list. While this may be instinctual for the best teams, many others lack the understanding and common language required to develop the habit of instilling and maintaining psychological safety and other core values. Along with clear, compelling objectives, creating the conversation with your team about the rules by which you will operate and cooperate is foundational and fundamental. Below is a quick two-part exercise that you can use to put the norms conversation on the table with your team:

Part I: Every Team Member

1. List your ideal team norms
2. List your current team norms
3. Identify any gaps

Part II: As a Team

1. Compare lists and gaps
2. What are our most important norms and significant gaps
3. What norms will we use to guide and assess behavior

I've never encountered an exceptional team that didn't make their values explicit and then use them to guide and assess behavior. Likewise, I've never worked with a mediocre or dysfunctional team that had established healthy norms and stuck with them. Make sure that you don't fall into the latter category

Element 2: Inspiring Motivation @ Work

"If your actions inspire others to dream more, learn more, do more, and become more, you are a leader." ~John Quincy Adams, 6th President of the United States

---

Motivation and engagement are popular topics during my many café conversations. Depending on whom I'm having coffee with (or, in my case, espresso) there are two recurring themes:

> Entrepreneurs and leaders of smaller, fast-growing companies often express their frustration, saying "The new people we've hired just don't

> seem to be as motivated as the people that have been here from the beginning, and some of them seem to be struggling."
>
> With team leaders in larger organizations that have formal engagement feedback programs I hear, "My engagement scores are too low, and nothing we do seems to move them very much."

While the symptoms of people lacking energy and engagement may be easy to identify, practical solutions that work can be hard to find. Search the web for "motivating teams" and you get: *25 Ways to Motivate Your Team to Greatness*, 15 *Effective Ways to Motivate Your Team*, and 10 *Unique Ways to Motivate Your Team*. In my experience, doing 25, 15, or even 10 different things to improve motivation isn't going to happen, and they're highly unlikely to work. When most days are like changing tires on a moving car, you just don't have the time to take on multiple changes, and you know that trying is more likely to result in a head-on collision rather than better performance.

From a behavioral science perspective, motivation is "energy that drives behavior for a purpose". When applied to the world of work, where people are striving to achieve specific outcomes, the phenomenon of motivation helps us understand what drives people to do what they do. As I noted earlier, one of the most widely tested and cross-culturally validated frameworks of motivation at work is self-determination theory (SDT). SDT describes the conditions under which people reach their potential and optimize their development and performance. It also identifies people's basic psychological needs for purpose, competence, and autonomy. Understanding those core needs is the key to improving the motivation of the people on your team. To get a deeper understanding of motivation at work and self-determination theory, see *Appendix C*.

Your objective as a leader is to coach each member of your team in finding meaning in their role, developing the competencies to achieve that end, and providing the appropriate level of autonomy to pursue it. It is crucial that each person can answer the question "what's my purpose?" in terms of both where they find personal meaning in their work, as well as how it aligns to the objectives and key results of the team and the broader organization. It is critical to balance these three components. If you allow imbalance, it causes motivation to deteriorate.

The Motivational Triangle™

In my workshops, people learn to create this balance with a simple tool called the Motivational Triangle. Visualize an equilateral triangle where each side represents a core psychological need. The length of each side of the triangle illustrates how fully each need is being satisfied. A person who has clarity of purpose in their work, has the competencies (or is supported in building them) to fulfill that purpose, and are given the appropriate amount of autonomy, has a balanced triangle.

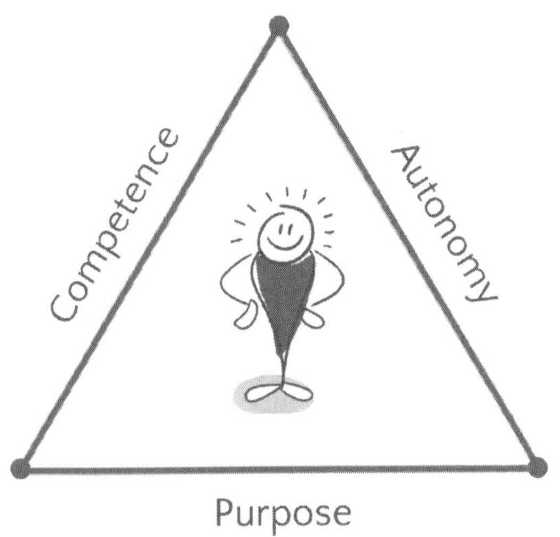

THE MOTIVATIONAL TRIANGLE™

In contrast, if a highly-competent person isn't getting the autonomy to pursue their purpose, they are being micromanaged. While someone who gets too much autonomy without clear purpose and enough skills, ends up stressed and burned out. In the latter two cases, the imbalance causes motivation to deteriorate.

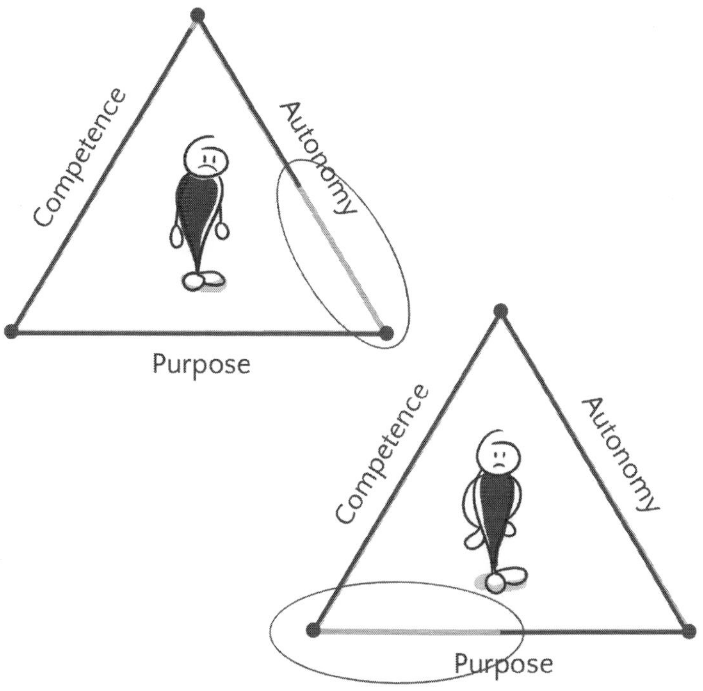

By identifying gaps in the length of the sides of the triangle for each team member, and taking steps to close those gaps, you can help maintain a high level of motivation.

Your first step is to build your own Motivational Triangle. Once you're comfortable doing so, you're ready to help others develop their Motivational Triangles and balance those needs to maximize their motivation at work:

- **Find Purpose.** It is essential that every team member has clarity in their role and the reason their role exists, and that they find real meaning in performing that work. Your goal is to gauge how clearly people understand the contribution their work makes to the goals of the team, the broader organization, and their own aspirations.
- **Develop Competencies.** There is a strong relationship between proficiency, confidence, and results. Your goal is to identify the capabilities that each person needs to achieve their purpose, and then gauge how fully they have developed those competencies.
- **Foster Autonomy.** Maximizing people's energy and engagement means they have the freedom to

The Basics of Motivation

Why we do what we do is one of the most interesting, complex, and perplexing questions for behavioral scientists, leaders, parents, and anyone else that deals with the mysteries of human motivation. A good starting point is to think about the conscious and non-conscious cognitive (thinking) and affective (emotional) drivers of our behavior. Our motivations—why we consciously or non-consciously do what we do—are governed by needs that range from the basic physiological (food, water, shelter, sex) to the needs for attachment/affiliation and autonomy. Those systems are strengthened or weakened in response to instinctive and learned response patterns (often from childhood) and our development over time. All these elements and themes come together to

> fulfill their purpose at work. That independence should be consistent with the clarity of their role and the level of their competencies. Your objective is to assess the degree of autonomy each team member needs to achieve their goals, versus their clarity of purpose, and level of competency.

The degree to which people satisfy their basic psychological needs determines whether people are turned on, or off, by their work. The process of fulfilling those needs helps people maximize what naturally, intrinsically motivates them, and identify the extrinsic elements of work that they wish to invest in and internalize. Building a high-performance 21st-century team means learning to resist the lists of pop-psychology quick-fixes and taking the time to understand the basic components of human motivation.

Motivating Across Cultures

I was recently conducting a one-hour executive review of the key concepts of crafting an extraordinary team. One of the participants from India asked, "Do you believe that there should be different approaches to leadership across cultures and organizational functions? Or does the Motivational Triangle enable us to use one

determine each person's unique 'inner theatre' and the narrative that defines who we are. One of the most important motivational concepts to understand and incorporate into coaching conversations is intrinsic vs. extrinsic motivation.

Intrinsic vs. Extrinsic Motivation

Visualize a spectrum with motivations that are part of our nature (intrinsic motivators) on one end, and those that originate outside of ourselves (extrinsic motivators) at the other end. Along the continuum are varying degrees to which an external source of motivation (for example, an idea) becomes more internalized as we begin to think of it as our own.

A typical two-year-old provides a great example of the intrinsic-to-extrinsic continuum. No one needs to teach a two-year-old the concept of play—it comes naturally, and the motivation to have fun is intrinsic. Whether they come across an empty box, a couple of sticks, or one of the endless number of toys available, most children will entertain themselves as long as their parents and attention spans allow. Conversely, I have never once come across a two-year-old who saw a toothbrush and toothpaste and decided it would be a great idea to place the latter on the former, put it in their mouth, and move it around for two minutes, every day, several times a day.

approach for everyone?" That's a great question, and the answer is two-fold:

First, differences in culture, as well as organizational function (for example sales versus R&D groups), matter when it comes to leader effectiveness. There is no one-size-fits-all approach. The way a leader works effectively with a local sales unit in China will differ from an R&D leader in India, Germany, Japan, or the United States. Good leadership takes into consideration the nuances that come with culture and area of responsibility.

Second, people's core psychological needs sit beneath cultural and organizational role influences. As humans, no matter where we're from or what we do, we all need to find meaning in our work, develop the competencies to fulfill that meaning, and feel as though we have the freedom to pursue our goals. The culture we come from, and our developmental experiences, influence how those core needs are expressed and met.

The Motivational Triangle is powerful because it enables you to use a single approach to understand both your own and your team members' core psychological needs, regardless of cultural context. You can then use those insights to inspire motivation in a culturally appropriate manner that works best for the people on your team. In the case of a global, virtual team, the Motiva-

Brushing our teeth is an idea and activity that begins as something external and controlled by parents. Only with coaxing, practice, and time does it become internalized and adopted as our own. From a motivational viewpoint, parents first help a child to find a reason for brushing their teeth (perhaps a bedtime story), to develop the skills to achieve that purpose (how to brush), and then allow them the independence to do it themselves as they come to internalize the idea. "Motivation at work" works much the same way.

Maslow and Motivation at Work

No discussion of the basics of motivation would be complete without mentioning Maslow's Hierarchy of Needs. First published in 1943, Maslow's basic premise at that time was that human needs form a hierarchy that is fulfilled in ascending order. Over the course of the next fifty-plus years Maslow's Hierarchy became a foundational element in virtually every Western basic psychology course. What is important to note is that this popularity is based more upon the intuitive appeal and an easy to understand pyramid versus substantive scientific evidence that supports it.

Key criticisms of Maslow's Hierarchy include questioning whether human needs are hierarchical; that the theory doesn't account for changing needs; and

tional Triangle enables you to reduce the need to be an expert in every culture.

Unraveling the mysteries of motivation at work, and understanding what really turns people on, isn't rocket science but it is behavioral science. Fortunately, when we narrow the context of motivation to "work", the answers to the question of "what we do" and "why" are less complex (and easier than motivating a two-year-old brush their teeth every night). For starters, the motivation to work, particularly when preceded by building advanced knowledge and skills, helps answer the fundamental "why" question. People who have set educational and experiential goals, and then put in the time and energy to meet them, have self-selected themselves into a group of people who desire to find a useful purpose for those competencies. This self-selection leaves you with the more manageable question of "how do I ensure that people are sufficiently motivated, energized, and engaged to do their best work?"

The Motivational Triangle helps you understand the state of the core needs of each team member, identify any gaps, and work together to close them. With that understanding, and by developing the habit of determining how well each person is satisfying their core needs, you are well positioned to inspire motivation at work.

that it is primarily a Western model versus universal. In his later years, Maslow himself revised his thinking and argued that self-actualization was not an automatic outcome of satisfying the other human needs in the pyramid. From a work motivation perspective, the biggest challenge with Maslow's Hierarchy is that it doesn't provide a practical means of using the theory in a real-world setting (try sitting down with someone on your team and creating a path to self-actualization).

Maslow got it right in terms of the role of core needs in motivation, and the power of a positive, humanistic approach to the psychology of motivation. Building upon those ideas, in the mid-1980's it was Deci and Ryan's Self-Determination theory (SDT) that identified a set of universal needs that, through approaches like The Motivational Triangle, can be used to inspire motivation in the day-to-day workplace.

Element 3: Team Relationship Coaching

"The best way to lead people into the future is to connect with them deeply in the present."
~James Kouzes and Barry Posner

Success in hyper-competitive, global markets demands that organizations tap into diverse skills, expertise, and experience. The realization of what can be accomplished when you put a group of great minds together has led to teams becoming the essential building block of organizations. The challenge is ensuring that people develop strong, trusting relationships, which enable adaptability and resilience in the face of constant change. Team relationship coaching focuses on key relationships and always includes:

- Gathering feedback about, and measuring the strength of, relationships between coworkers, between team members and their leader, and across supporting groups.
- Identifying gaps before they lead to conflict, deteriorating performance, and disengagement.

- Understanding and influencing team processes and behaviors to improve performance and promote well-being.

Relationship coaching is founded on the experience-expectation dynamic that exists between people who work together to achieve a goal. That dynamic is built upon four pillars of behavioral science: Engagement Theory, Self-Determination Theory, Psychological Contract Theory, and Expectancy Disconfirmation Theory. You can read about these theories in the *Glossary*.

From a relationship coaching perspective, it's important to understand that we, as humans, have an expectation of every single experience. Moreover, we associate a level of feeling (affect) with every experience and assign a (cognitive) level of importance to it. The significance we place on the experience, versus the level of our expectation, determines the energy and emotion that we associate with that experience, as well as any gaps. For example, you may have a high expectation of the quality of the espresso at your favorite café. If one afternoon your experience falls short of that expectation, you may be mildly irritated, but (hopefully) it doesn't ruin your day. On the other hand, if your spouse or significant other has a high expectation of you for an upcoming anniversary, and you deliver an experience well below that expectation, the repercussions will likely be emotional and last for a while. You can measure any relationship in the context of the experience-expectation dynamic:

- If your experience meets or exceeds your expectations, how does it make you feel? How does it affect the level of energy and engagement you express in that relationship?
- If your experience falls short of your expectations, how does that affect your energy and level of engagement?

Our experiences versus our expectations affect the state of our relationships: are we engaged or disengaged; is our relationship developing or deteriorating. Measuring, understanding, and closing experience-expectation gaps is essential to building and sustaining highly-effective teams. Identifying and closing disparities between what we expect of our key relationships and what we experience taps into the essence of humanity that powers energy and engagement at work. Over the past few years, I've talked with scores of leaders that found themselves dealing with the effect of experience-expectation gaps that impeded performance, energy, and engagement—and I've experienced the impact first hand.

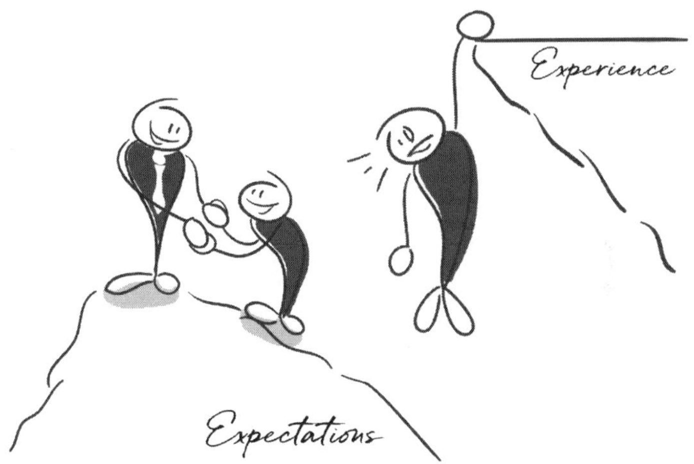

By the fall of 2017, I was beginning the last year of my work leading teams at HP. With my doctorate in hand, three successful leadership assignments behind me, and good results with the dozens of teams I had worked with across Asia-Pacific, I felt ready for any challenge. I was then asked to take on what turned out to be one of the most difficult, and interesting, team leadership challenges of my career.

Earlier, during the summer of 2017, a new division was formed by the merger of three existing product categories. The product lines ranged in life-cycle maturity from newly emerging to mature/end-of-life, and the people involved—along with the cultures they came from—were equally diverse. The GM of the new division asked if I would lead those product category teams and the business group, while focusing on overall team excellence. As he and I held similar views about leadership, especially the importance of shared leadership, the fit seemed to be ideal. What neither of us anticipated was the degree of difference in people's values, gaps in their competencies, and significant trust issues. Compounding those issues, we were asked to deliver financial results that turned out to be at odds with the reality of people's capabilities, product readiness, and customer buying cycles.

At first, it was rough going. The pressure to deliver sales drove dysfunctional behaviors in some of the country sales units, leading to poor decision making and inaccurate communications internally and to customers. We saw the destructive powers of gossip, with negative comments quickly infecting team members across the region. In addition, several of the regional team members were overwhelmed by the broader scope of responsibilities. The GM and I were under significant pressure to intervene and manage the details of the business—but we resisted and stayed true to our belief that the key to long-term success was crafting a robust and resilient team capable of shared leadership. To do that we needed to coach, not command.

By mid-2018 we addressed the most serious issues by removing a 'lone wolf' who had turned toxic as a country team leader, and reinforcing the value that anyone can talk about anybody as long as it is positive. It's worth noting the importance of establishing positive norms versus one's that forbid behaviors. Setting the bar high and helping people get there is far more powerful than telling people what not to do. We also swapped the roles of two key team members to better align their skills and began intensive coaching with several others. Those actions closed the most significant expectation gaps between the regional business and country sales groups. Good progress in a few months, but at that point in the year we also knew that we would not achieve our budget targets for the full year.

Underachieving business goals is always a serious matter as it impacts both reported results and people's paychecks. While neither the GM nor I felt good about where we stood at mid-year versus the annual budget, we could also see changes happening that, over the coming 12 months, would lead to a dramatic improvement in performance. While we never gave up on pursuing every possible deal during the rest of the fiscal year, we kept coaching people to close gaps among themselves and with our customers. Fiscal Year 2018 ended with the disappointing results we predicted, but with a team poised to thrive. A quarter into the new year, they were well ahead of their sales targets for both the quarter and the first half and were heading for a stellar FY2019. Most importantly, despite being spread out across the Asia-Pacific region, the people learned to communicate and collaborate through a combination of shared leadership and developing the habit of consistently closing experience-expectation gaps. Moreover, they embraced the ideal that only the group performs, and the individual members contribute to this performance.

The reality for most teams is days overloaded with meetings, ad-hoc tasks, and looming deadlines. When the situation turns difficult, it's tempting for leaders to try and tackle every problem and manage every issue themselves. High-performance teams take the opposite approach, allowing each team member to take ownership for successes and failures. While there are no magic wands or quick fixes when it comes to team excellence, the key habit that establishes the path to excellence is focusing on relationship coaching and addressing the most significant experience-expectation gaps impeding effectiveness. By managing team relationships, you have built the foundation to coach your teams with confidence.

Chapter Highlights

- The tension between the drive for productivity and efficiency, and the needs of employees, defined management thinking throughout the 20th century.
- The quest for balance between the "things of production" and the "humanity of production," was spearheaded early in the century by luminaries like Abraham Maslow and Douglas McGregor.
- In the latter part of the century, psychologists Edward Deci and Richard Ryan uncovered the conditions under which people realize their potential and optimize their development, performance, and well-being.
- The highly-dynamic, and at times chaotic, nature of teamwork in a complex global (and often virtual) environment requires tremendous adaptability and resiliency.
- TRM is an approach to improving the performance of teams in that chaotic environment, along with the well-being of the individuals on the team.

- The TRM architecture consists of three elements:
    - Team Relationship Fundamentals: establishing the clarity of purpose and healthy norms that are critical to creating a highly-functional culture
    - Inspiring Individual Motivation: understanding the psychological needs that, when met, inspire and energize people to do their best for themselves and the team
    - Team Relationship Coaching: the core leadership practice that drives team effectiveness and well-being
- In its essence, TRM is a set of practices that offer what may be the single most significant opportunity for organizations to ensure that their teams are able to innovate and compete in the 21st century.

Thoughts & Notes

Thoughts & Notes

Establish Your Team Purpose

1. Develop a set of specific objectives and key results that align with the broader unit or organization goals.
2. Identify the key relationships, as well as the formal and informal communications processes, necessary to accomplish the goals of the team.
3. Describe the context in which the team will operate. For example, a global virtual, a co-located, or a permanent functional team.
4. List the key competencies people must have to be successful in delivering the team goals. Identify any gaps/areas to strengthen.
5. Reflecting on the goals, relationships, context, and competencies from the first four steps, develop a two- to three-sentence team purpose statement. Make sure it's clear and compelling.

Thoughts & Notes

Thoughts & Notes

Develop YourTeam Norms

To develop your team norms, have every team member do the following:

1. List your ideal team norms
2. List your current team norms
3. Identify any gaps

Then, as a team sit down and discuss the following:

1. Compare lists and gaps
2. What are our most important norms and significant gaps
3. What norms will we use to guide and assess behavior

Thoughts & Notes

Thoughts & Notes

Motivational Triangle

Use the template on the opposite page to create your own Motivational Triangle. Each side of the triangle represents a core psychological need. Draw how fully each need is being satisfied.

For each core need, identify any gaps, then write out what actions you need to take to close those gaps.

Purpose:

Competence:

Autonomy:

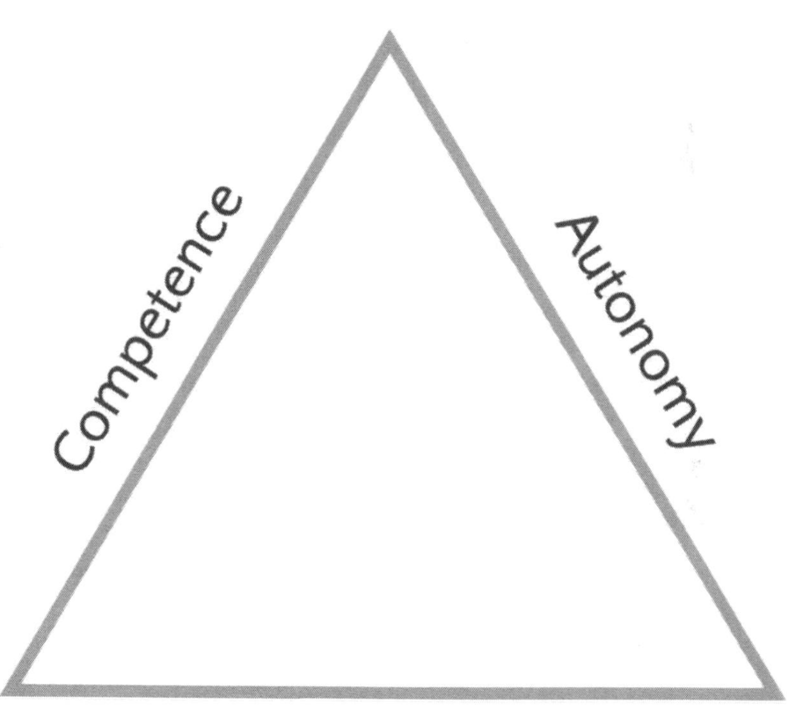
Competence
Autonomy
Purpose

Thoughts & Notes

Experience-Expectation Gaps

What are the most significant experience-expectation gaps on your team?

Thoughts & Notes

The Core of TRM: Coaching Your Team

"The way to achieve your own success is to be willing to help somebody else get it first."

~Iyanla Vanzant

When I described the third element of the TRM architecture (Team Relationship Coaching) in the previous chapter, I emphasized that, while there are no magic wands or quick fixes when it comes to team excellence, team relationship coaching is the one habit that sustains a foundation of team excellence. In this chapter, we'll do a deep dive into the foundations and practices of relationship coaching. Topics include the importance of feedback, measuring relationship strength—especially across virtual teams, and creating effective coaching conversations. However, before jumping into "how" you implement, we'll start with "why?"

Why relationship coaching? If you haven't asked yourself that question, you should. Good coaching requires a substantial commitment of time and energy. Moreover, it requires experience and wisdom to help develop other people. Most team leaders, especially new leaders, find themselves short on time, and coaching-wisdom is often still a primordial soup waiting to be shaped by experiences yet to come. That said, coaching others is worth the investment—regardless of your lack of time or experience.

Why? Because, typically, people are only willing to fully engage when they feel a sense of identity and belonging within a community that has a shared purpose and culture. In their study *How Millennials Want to Work and Live,* Gallup asked millennials about their expectations of engaging with their boss. The answer was that they don't want bosses, they want coaches. And, they don't want annual reviews, they want ongoing conversations. Conversely, without coaching, it can be an enormous challenge to get talented people to work effectively with one another. That takes trust and respect which must be earned over time, not commanded from above. An investment in developing your relationship coaching skills pays dividends long after you've moved on from your current role.

The answer to 'why?' also comes in the form of the pain that most everyone has experienced at some point in their career—the damage done by mediocre or incompetent people sitting in leadership positions. People evolve primarily through experience. Coaching provides the opportunity to craft an experiential-learning environment while developing people who are able (and motivated) to benefit from the effort. In parallel, you will untether people's creativity and gain a critical development experience for yourself. When you consider the cost in both human and economic terms of lousy leadership and disengaged people—and the possibilities that come with extraordinary leaders and teams—the answer to 'why coach' becomes crystal clear.

One of the most powerful insights that emerged from my research on team effectiveness was that every exceptional leader developed expertise in the art of fostering strong, trusting relationships—while few, if any, mediocre leaders place much emphasis or value on team relationship coaching. I uncovered an assortment of reasons for this difference in people's behavior, ranging from the nature of the work to dysfunctional company cultures that ignore—or even penalize—any priority other than delivering bottom-line results. However, what got in the way most often was someone's unwillingness or inability to reflect upon how their habits were encouraging or inhibiting the development of their team.

Professor Amy Edmondson has made teams her academic focus. She eloquently makes the point, "Great teams consist of individuals who have learned to trust each other. Over time, they have discovered each other's strengths and weaknesses, enabling them to play as a coordinated whole." In *Team of Teams,* General McChrystal accentuates Edmondson's point, writing that, "SEAL teams accomplish remarkable feats not simply because of the individual qualifications of their members, but because those members coalesce into a single organism. Such oneness is not inevitable, nor is it a fortunate coincidence. The SEALs forge it methodically and deliberately... Without this trust, SEAL teams would just be a collection of fit soldiers. BUD/S [SEAL basic training and qualification] builds trust between members, beginning with the seemingly arbitrary demands to walk to meals together and ending (for those who complete training) with SEALs willing to place their lives in one another's hands."

It would be the unusual (and likely career-limited) leader who would admit that they don't aspire to build energized, engaged teams that deliver exceptional performance. Yet, results often fall short of aspirations. When I ask people about the discrepancy between their aspirations and reality, they give a variety of reasons for their performance. A few leaders are reflective and introspective and 'own the gap'; most describe a series of factors outside their control that lead to disappointing results.

From a behavioral perspective, attributing external causes as the primary reason for poor performance is nothing new. Car owners regularly demonstrate this behavior. When surveyed, 93% of US drivers rate themselves as being better than average. When presented with their track record of driving mishaps, people are quick to blame other drivers, bad weather, poor road conditions, or other external causes. The root of this behavior, known as a cognitive bias, explains the common tendency for people to see themselves as superior, despite evidence to the contrary (a.k.a. a superiority bias). That is not to diminish the impact of outside forces. External factors can influence outcomes and should be recognized—and a little cognitive bias can help build self-confidence. However, a strong superiority bias, left unchecked, inhibits continuous improvement and sustained performance.

It is our habits—conscious and subconscious—that put us (and our teams) on the path to excellence or allow us to meander into complacency. As a leader, you must invest in a mental mirror wherein you can examine your habits and reflect on what you aspire to do versus what you actually do. Over the years I've had the opportunity to work with some especially performance-driven sales groups. Their self-confidence and will-to-win were unmatched. In some cases, the strength of the team's cognitive superiority bias and their ability to distort reality was also unmatched. The leaders chose not to invest time into reflecting on results, whether good or bad. Their focus was on pushing ever harder to deliver the next quarter. For a time, it worked. Until it didn't. Once they hit that tipping point, no amount of spin could hide the gap between the way the leaders saw themselves and their team, versus the business results.

In contrast, during my research into exceptional teams, I also had the opportunity to spend time with performance-driven teams who were equally dedicated to reflection as well as continuously closing any discrepancies between aspiration and action. During one memorable evening with a group of Israeli Air Force (IAF) fighter pilots, they described their approach to preventing superiority biases. It was as simple as it was challenging. After every mission, they held an After-Action Review. For any gap or variance in performance, there was one point of responsibility, one squadron member who owned the gap, and stood in front of his peers and superiors to answer three questions: What was the gap? Why was there a gap? How to close the gap?

No excuses. No reality distortions. Total ownership.

One pilot summed up the process saying, "You have to understand, that to do our job, we must believe that we are the best-of-the-best. But, if that confidence becomes arrogance to the point that we stop improving, and we aren't 100% honest with ourselves and our squadron about any gap or issue, then someone may not come home from the next mission".

For leaders who have grown comfortable in organizations where distorting reality to explain and rationalize mediocre performance is part of the culture, the reflection in the mirror can be uncomfortable, even psychologically painful. Often those leaders' egos have become entwined with their position. When their effectiveness in that position is questioned, even by themselves, it threatens their egos and associated sense of worth. This anxiety makes developing the habit of recognizing biases, and candidly reflecting on the behaviors that get in the way of learning and improvement, a significant challenge. Mastering that challenge requires leaders to own any gap and rigorously pursue the answers to the three questions: What is the gap? Why is there a gap? and How do I close the gap?

Overcoming biases and developing exceptional coaching habits is hard. If it were easy, everyone would do it, especially given the rewards of team performance and engagement. Instead, many leaders unintentionally choose mediocrity. The fact that a choice may be subconscious doesn't make it any less a choice. Returning to the example of the IAF fighter pilots acknowledging the risk, exceptional leaders put their issues and choices on the table and own them. No excuses. No reality distortions. Regularly examining your habits is the first big step to becoming an exceptional coach and will go a long way to ensure that you put your people on the path to excellence and keep them there.

At the heart of great team-coaching is the quality of the relationships between people. Do it right, and you will create a vibrant, diverse group where talented people are committed to one another and passionate about their work. Moreover, when you set the stage for people to be a part of creating something extraordinary, they will make your team a magnet for talented people.

The Breakfast of Champions

"In teamwork, silence isn't golden, it's deadly."~Mark Sanborn

---

During my first experience as a team leader, I had a great manager whose leadership development practices were well ahead of the times. In an era of annual reviews and forced rankings, he was a coach who set the bar high then supported his people to reach it. He continuously checked-in with me and the other product managers and used our mistakes as opportunities to help us grow as leaders. He also set a requirement to regularly seek input from my team on how I could improve. Being young and inexperienced, I knew I was making plenty of mistakes, so the idea of asking my direct reports for feedback (and worse, sharing it with my boss!) was a little terrifying. Reality turned out to be quite different. As I made it a habit to gather regular feedback, the effect on my team's performance and their job satisfaction was so positive that I quickly became addicted to the practice.

Since that first experience, and despite the overwhelming evidence that supports the connection between seeking constructive feedback and people's effectiveness and well-being, I've learned that I wasn't alone in my initial "feedback anxiety." Jim Kouzes and Barry Posner, co-authors of the book *The Leadership Challenge: How to Make Extraordinary Things Happen in Organizations,* developed a widely used behavioral assessment for leaders: The Leadership Practices Inventory. Across more than one million assessments, one factor consistently receives the absolute lowest rating: "[my team leader] asks for feedback on how his/her actions affect other people's performance."

Over more than twenty-five years, I've coached leaders to reach out to their teams and peers for feedback—and most of the time, they cringe at the idea. The habit of seeking feedback may not be easy to develop, but failing to seek honest input from your team can lead to reduced psychological safety, loss of trust, the deterioration of relationships, and ultimately disengagement. The impact on performance and well-being carries a heavy price.

So why do some leaders choose to avoid feedback, even when they have ample evidence that shows its benefits? Part of the answer can be found by looking at the impact of feedback in the context of the Motivational Triangle and the three universal psychological needs that drive motivation and well-being at work:

- Purpose is what gets us out of bed every day believing that we are doing something worthwhile. Feedback can either strengthen the belief that we are making a significant impact or shatter it.
- Competence is our ability to perform the day-to-day tasks we perform as we pursue our purpose. Competence is also at the heart of self-confidence. When feedback doesn't match what we perceive as our capabilities, it can motivate us to change, or it might crush our confidence.
- Autonomy is our innate drive to exercise control over our role and priorities at work to accomplish

> our purpose. Feedback is essential to balancing the freedom to pursue our purpose with our ability to handle that level of independence based upon our competencies.

When those three needs are aligned and being met, people find themselves energized and engaged by their work, and open to feedback to continue to improve. For leaders, the challenge is that with greater responsibility comes an expectation of greater capabilities. As they internalize those expectations, and as they begin to judge themselves—or see themselves as judged by others—on those expectations, the stage is set for a leader to choose the dark comfort of ignorance rather than dealing with the light of critical feedback.

I witnessed this a few years ago when the head of a division moved to a new role. Her replacement was highly-motivated, but very inexperienced and lacked some of the basic competencies necessary as a leader. The new GM found great meaning in his new role and was driven to make a difference, but the gaps in his leadership capabilities caused him to be highly sensitive to what he saw as potential damage to his image. He saw feedback as drawing attention to this lack of experience, causing him not only to avoid asking for feedback but proactively discouraging it. The result was, unfortunately, predictable—both the performance of the division and the well-being of the people suffered for years until he moved on to a new role.

The draw to remain in the dark comfort of ignorance is powerful when the bright light of feedback feels like a threat to your self-image or your legitimacy in a role. The habit of seeking feedback develops as you understand and address the root cause of feedback anxiety—the level of psychological safety you experience within your organization. Psychological safety, the "shared belief that a team will not embarrass, reject, or punish someone for speaking up," enables people to feel they can trust others and be themselves. More importantly, psychological safety is a two-way street, which applies to the leader as much as it does to members of the team. If you are like most leaders, then you're sensitive to the high expectations that come with your role. If you feel judged or criticized when receiving feedback, it's natural to prefer staying in the dark versus risking your self-image. Just like the GM's aversion to feedback had its roots in an organizational culture that was psychologically unsafe, he perpetuated that lack of psychological safety through his behavior. Expectations were set very high, coaching was almost non-existent, and people were quick to criticize.

Establishing a psychologically-safe culture requires you to encourage feedback and build a team environment in which everyone sees shedding light on areas to improve as an opportunity rather than a threat. Only when you and your people feel safe to express yourselves will you avoid the dark and fully embrace feedback and self-assessment.

For organizations such as Amazon, Deloitte, and Facebook, feedback plays a leading role in developing and sustaining the cultures that champion high-performance and employee welfare.

Amazon

In an interview, Beth Galetti (Amazon's Senior Vice President of Worldwide Human Resources) discussed the role of cultural values at Amazon, emphasizing the critical role they played as the company grew to over 500,000 employees. She called out the importance of Amazon's Leadership Principles, characterizing them as, "...the living embodiment of our culture, regardless of job role or geographic location". Key among those Leadership Principles is to "earn trust", which focuses on communications and feedback. Leaders are expected to listen attentively, speak candidly, and treat others respectfully. Summarizing the role and importance of

Brain Science Turns Feedback Inside-Out

Employee surveys emerged in the 1920s, along with scientific management and the drive to improve industrial productivity. In 1932, Rensis Likert began a revolution in survey research with the publication of his article "A Technique for the Measurement of Attitudes." Likert argued that, while human attitudes are infinite, they can be clustered together and the questions that emerge from those clusters can be scored on a simple one-to-five scale. Research into the psychology of group dynamics during and after World War II increased the use of employee attitude measurement tools. The United States Army Research Branch alone surveyed more than half a million soldiers on topics ranging from food quality to confidence in leadership. Today, with the help of the Internet and companies like Survey Monkey (who claim to have deployed over 100 million surveys), employee attitude surveys have reached pandemic proportions

Deloitte's Human Capital Trends survey identified "teamwork" as the number one global workforce trend. Around the world, employees today are expected to work collaboratively and interdependently in networks of project teams—and central to their success is continuous feedback. For individuals, feedback improves awareness of strengths and

feedback, Beth noted, "We favor straightforward, two-way communications. When we talk about our work, we use plain language and specific examples over generalizations and corporate-speak".

Deloitte

In their HBR article, "Reinventing Performance Management", Marcus Buckingham and Ashley Goodall described the redesign of Deloitte's performance management system. One of the key objectives of the redesign was to fuel team performance. Deloitte's research into the practices of the best team leaders revealed that they conduct weekly check-ins with each team member about short-term work. These brief, feedback-oriented conversations provide an opportunity to align purpose, expectations, and progress on short-term outcomes. For Deloitte, the feedback and discussions created by the check-ins came to define the essence of a team leader's work. In their testing, Deloitte found a direct and measurable correlation between check-ins and engagement.

Facebook

In the HBR article, "Employee Surveys Are Still One of the Best Ways to Measure Engagement", Scott Judd,

weaknesses and provides insights on how to self-correct behavior. For leaders, frequent, high-quality feedback is like radar for your team. It identifies gaps—such as trust issues, unconscious bias, disregard for equal voice, or a lack of psychological safety—on and across teams before they lead to deteriorating performance and disengagement.

When developed and used properly, employee surveys provide a powerful tool for both predicting behaviors and creating transformational coaching conversations. Unfortunately, most fall short of providing the feedback that is most needed for modern team success. While the majority of surveys have moved online, most still use methods designed for a paper-pencil era. Often, they are Do-It-Yourself questionnaires designed by a well-intended HR person using practices such as the 16 guidelines for content, format, language, measurement, and administration offered in the HBR article "Getting the Truth into Workplace Surveys". Without research and design expertise, the result is usually too many questions, with biases that diminish the validity of the results. More significantly, the global survey epidemic has resulted in survey fatigue and devaluation as the number of issues raised usually exceeds the ability of an organization to address them. The result? People feel their voice isn't recognized or the organization doesn't care to address

Eric O'Rourke, and Adam Grant describe the results of internal research at Facebook on employee feedback. They highlighted three principal reasons why the company places a strong emphasis on gathering and responding to feedback:

1. Feedback is predictive. They found that asking people about turn-over intent was more accurate than machine-learning and predictive analytics.
2. Feedback feels good. The act of giving feedback gives employees a means of expressing voice.
3. Feedback facilitates change. Listening is a bidirectional process, fostering learning and influence.

Scott, Eric, and Adam acknowledged that technology and analytics will continue to play an important role in managing and developing people, but they remind us that the human dimension of feedback surveys will only make them more important in a world of algorithms.

Few people would be surprised that Amazon, Deloitte, and Facebook's approach to team development and performance differs from the average organization, or that they share employee feedback and follow-up best practices in common. The idea that feedback is good—and responding to it is even better—is almost cliché. But why is feedback so vital that some of the world's most

their real concerns, which sets up a cycle of diminishing input quality. This is happening at a time when robust feedback is more critical than ever for team success and personal satisfaction. The key question for team leaders is how to regularly gather insights into what really drives team behavior, effectiveness, and well-being—all without triggering survey fatigue and poor-quality feedback.

Applied Brain Science is Turning Surveys "Inside-Out"

The "inside-out" approach to employee surveys allows people to provide feedback that highlights what is most important to them. The survey tools and methods developed for 20th-century organizations are far less applicable in today's team-based, knowledge-driven businesses. A traditional Likert scale attitudinal survey takes an "outside-in" survey-centric approach. Looking in from the outside, the survey developers make assumptions about the most important employee topics—like engagement, perks, training, and culture—and the right questions to ask using a simple scoring scale. To avoid missing an issue assumed to be important by HR or managers, developers take a shotgun approach with dozens of questions. In addition to creating survey fatigue, the "rate this one to five" or "Very Unsatisfied to Very Satisfied" approach fails to

successful companies make it a core part of their culture?

Looking below the surface to the psychological drivers that make feedback, and a leader's response to it, important demonstrates why it plays a vital role in increasing performance and satisfaction. Feedback is an essential ingredient in meeting the core psychological needs that inspire motivation at work.

- Through coaching, feedback helps people find a connection with, and purpose in, their work.
- Feedback is crucial for developing people's competencies so they can fulfill their purpose.
- Continuous feedback ensures that the level of autonomy your team members need to pursue their purpose matches their ability to handle that level of independence.

Meeting those core needs depends upon a continual dialog between you and your team, as well as between teammates. Feedback also sits at the center of building the interpersonal dynamics that are essential for healthy relationships. The core dynamic in any relationship is the expectations we have versus our experiences. Unresolved experience-expectation differences lead to grievances, relationship deterioration, and ultimately disengagement. Getting feedback, and closing those

uncover the more complex issues that can dramatically affect team effectiveness and well-being.

The 21st-century alternative is an "inside-out" approach that starts with a people-centric point of view. This approach assumes that, in the context of their organization, team, and specific goals, employees can best identify what is most important to their well-being and effectiveness. By asking questions that encourage people to express how they think and feel about what is helping (or hindering) them to achieve their goals, a survey can get to the heart of what does or doesn't motivate, energize, and engage them. How to do this requires drawing upon a more modern foundation of research and practice at the intersection of behavioral science, neuroscience, and design. Behavioral science demonstrates the power of focusing on understanding a person's experience versus their expectation relative to a goal and across the relationships that are important to achieving that goal. Developing a feedback survey from the "inside-out"—capturing people's experience versus their expectation and the reason for any gap—provides immediate insights into the most critical issues that are supporting or interfering with effectiveness and well-being.

Neuroscience research shows the critical importance of capturing both affective (emotions) and cogni-

gaps, heals relationships.

A few years ago, I encountered a situation that demonstrated the healing power of that experience-expectation dynamic. A division Vice President at a New York-based materials science and manufacturing company was having challenges with performance and turnover on one of his R&D teams. He implemented a feedback process that captured team member expectations of one-another, versus their expectations, and measured and mapped relationship strength. The approach quickly uncovered the root cause of the issues: subconscious gender bias. Women didn't feel that they were being treated as equals, pointing out that they were often talked-over or had their ideas ignored, and often felt that their voice didn't matter. With the VP's guidance, the team addressed the issue and agreed on two norms:

- We will work to see and eliminate bias.
- Everyone is responsible for ensuring psychological safety and team equality.

Identifying the issues, putting them on the table, and dealing with them openly prevented the departure of a top engineer. Within six months, the team had resolved the turnover issues and saw a marked improvement in their performance metrics.

tive (thinking) feedback. Despite these insights, most survey methods used today were developed in the early 20th century and don't provide an effective means of doing so. The neuroscience bridge to 21st-century surveys is facial expressions, as they are one of the most vital cues in both affective and cognitive communication. Extensive research into human-computer interaction demonstrates that emoticons (or emoji) are an effective way to make up for many of the cues absent in text-based communications. Well-designed interactive emoticons mimic facial expressions and foster the expression of feelings. These should form the core of an "inside-out" employee survey.

Interactive survey design can combine the "inside-out" experience-expectation questions that uncover the key issues interfering with people's performance and happiness, with emoji facial expression animation that enables greater emotional expressiveness and makes the survey itself more engaging. The result is a comprehensive picture of a team's experience, energy, and engagement while eliminating survey fatigue and encouraging frequent use.

Moving from an "outside-in" to an "inside-out" approach when developing employee surveys allows people to provide feedback that highlights what is most important to them and identifies the

Exceptional leaders and their teams don't treat feedback as an activity to be added to already busy workdays; seeking feedback and proactively responding to it is a habit that forms an integral part of a leader's role. It is an essential practice of the best teams and organizations.

It is critical that you muster the courage to seek feedback —and take timely action based upon that feedback. The key to making feedback your 'breakfast of champions' is by ensuring psychological safety and framing feedback as learning, versus evaluation and judgment. When you make feedback a habit, you encourage a stronger sense of purpose, leading to greater team effectiveness and improved well-being.

Relationship Metrics

"In business, the idea of measuring what you are doing, picking the measurements that count... you thrive on that." ~Bill Gates

---

most significant gaps that are getting in the way of their being productive and happy. Adopting insights from modern brain science ensures that surveys capture both how people feel and what they think, producing richer and more predictive insights. And good design can put the pieces together in a compelling and engaging way that ensures a continuous flow of extensive feedback that leads to more meaningful team conversations.

From Peter Drucker's mantra "If you can't measure it, you can't improve it." and processes like six-sigma, to big-data analytics and people metrics of all types, the underlying (and well supported) premise is that, through better data and metrics, organizations can improve their performance. In parallel, teams have risen to dominate the organizational landscape as the preferred, if not essential means, by which companies innovate and compete. Yet, despite teams playing a critical role in the future of most organizations, few leaders measure the most critical predictors of effectiveness over time—the health of the relationships on and across teams.

At a start-up, where team effectiveness can mean life-or-death for the company, measuring relationship strength and acting quickly to close gaps is a survival tool. In the tech sector, young companies grow rapidly, and focusing on team excellence can take a back-seat to activities like business development and funding. Relationship metrics give CEOs and investors a means of mitigating risk as well as a forward-looking, predictive tool to help gauge the probability of success. At large, global organizations, relationship metrics flag people issues and help tear down silos by cultivating trust across geographies and cultures. By measuring both relationship strength and experience versus expectation gaps, and identifying who's working on closing them, you'll keep people aligned and foster open, candid relationships both vertically and horizontally.

Relationship metrics are like radar for your team—allowing you to identify issues before they lead to deteriorating performance and disengagement. The relationship metrics that you should be using are:

1. Experience-expectation gaps. A measure of the size of any differences between each team member's expectations versus their experience with peers; with you the team leader; and with other teams who support them in achieving their goals.
2. Team relationship strength. An aggregate, comparable measure of relationship strength. Highly-positive experiences with high expectations are the basis for strong relationships, while negative experiences or low expectations characterize weak or impaired relationships. Neutral relationships don't have a substantial impact on other people's experiences, either positive or negative.

Making a habit of tracking any actions taken to close experience-expectation issues and improve relationship strength is the key to increasing team effectiveness and improving personal well-being. This is especially true for the dramatically increasing number of global, virtual teams.

Relationships Across Virtual Teams

Virtual teams often face greater complexity and uncertainty as they strive to overcome the barriers of time, distance, and communications. When successful, virtual teams enable the best talent to come together to amplify energy, competencies, and creativity. However, with increased geographical, time zone, and cultural distances, the challenges to developing highly-effective virtual teams are significant. Research shows the critical importance of ensuring that people on virtual teams have a shared understanding of the team's goals and that leaders develop and maintain strong trusting relationships. Your challenge is developing trust and understanding among virtual team members who have limited opportunity to interact face-to-face with you or other people on the team.

Virtual Team Metrics at Google

In early April 2019, Veronica Gilrane, People Analytics Manager at Google and leader of the People Innovation Lab (PiLab) conducted a study within Google to better understand the impact of virtual teamwork. With over 100,000 people spread across 150 cities and more than 50 countries, a significant amount of work must be accomplished with people that don't bump into each other in the hallway. The PiLab research showed that 48% of meetings involved people from two or more campus building sites; 39% two or more cities; and 30% of meetings happen across two or more time zones.

The PiLab team sent surveys to more than 5000 employees globally and held focus groups with another hundred people around the world to better understand the impact and implications of virtual work. They measured factors such as well-being, performance, and connectedness. Unsurprisingly, staying connected across time zones and cultures can make establishing connections more difficult. The team's recommendations focused on a few key areas:

Establish rapport. Team leaders that engage in informal conversation before jumping into the business at hand help co-workers to get to know each other as people and build human connections that impact effectiveness and welfare.

Establish rules and boundaries. Don't assume. Ask the team for feedback and the rules by which they will operate, including the optimal time for meetings.

Balance face-to-face and virtual. Leaders should lay out clear guidelines for in-person meetings and create opportunities at key times to establish those face-to-face connections.

Establish healthy norms. It is especially important on video/virtual calls that the leader establishes team values and rules, such as ensuring psychological safety and equal voice, and then use those rules to guide behavior —for example by making sure that they visibly acknowledge people's contributions.

Google prides itself on its extraordinary teams. Research like that conducted by the PiLab provides leaders with metrics and recommendations that help to ensure that there are no differences in the effectiveness, well-being, or career opportunities for virtual team members.

One of the more interesting business development assignments I took on during my five-year immersion in teamwork at HP was crafting a region-wide team to grow one of the core consumables businesses. The makeup of the unit consisted of a headquarters group in Singapore, and country teams in Japan, China, Korea, India, South East Asia, and Australia/New Zealand. The initial challenges included misaligned goals across HQ functions, inconsistent business practices across countries (resulting in wildly different margins) with a lot of top-down pressure to fix margins quickly, and country-team resistance towards any change suggestions by HQ. Adding to the challenge, I had just brought on a new Regional Category Manager who came with exceptional financial and analytical talent, but no experience in Asia or in leading a cross-cultural virtual team. The challenges were clear, but the answers were not.

The temptation was to take a top-down approach and go after the seemingly 'low hanging fruit' of inconsistent margins. The strong finance background of our Category Manager (and the pressure from regional leadership) added to that temptation. But, we resisted and committed to exceeding our margin and revenue goals within 18-months. The ensuing months became a demonstration of the power of shared-leadership, trust-building, and the importance of relationship metrics. After first visiting each country, the Category Manager brought all the groups to Singapore. Rather than hours of regional presentations as was the usual practice, he presented one slide with our current P&L and our 18-month business goals. We spent the next three days working with each team on ideas to reach those goals, and, in the process, ensuring that everyone was in line with them. In parallel, we began measuring the variation between people's experience and their expectations of each other and identifying the associated issues. The issues, and the steps we took to address them, were reviewed with all team members every six weeks.

Those two actions—establishing clear, compelling shared goals and consistently identifying, measuring, and closing relationship gaps—were the catalysts that energized people to meet their goals within the 18 months. Just as significantly, as the level of people's engagement increased and the strength of their relationships improved, so did the number of innovative ideas and the speed of implementation.

Building trust and understanding across time zones and cultures requires you to amp up your team radar—frequently gathering feedback from all team members on their expectations versus their actual experiences, measuring and understanding any disparities, and continuously closing them. Most importantly, virtual team leaders must ensure a culture that supports a high-degree of conversation equality and psychological safety. Early warning of any breakdown in understanding or trust is essential to preventing the deterioration that leads to disengagement.

The nature of team leadership is rapidly changing as you are tasked with building teams in increasingly flat organizations that operate across generational, cultural, and geographic boundaries. As organizations become more dependent on teams for their success, your ability to identify potential issues before they diminish performance and engagement has become more critical than ever. Turning on your radar, and using it to measure and track the health of key relationships, adds a critical capability that is missing on most teams.

Creating Effective Coaching Conversations

"Make sure that team members know they are working with you, not for you."
~John Wooden

If you've ever played the game of golf, you quickly realized that there are countless ways to hit the ball wrong (I believe that I've experienced nearly every one of them) and far fewer ways to achieve a consistently good result. Coaching conversations are much the same. There are so many ways to create conversations that range from awkward to disastrous, that finding a consistently effective approach can be a challenge. The common question asked by both golfers and team leaders is: How do I improve my game? Golfers, whether weekend duffer or tour professional, can turn to a multi-billion-dollar industry that combines ever-evolving equipment with coaching tips and techniques that take advantage of the latest technology. For most new leaders, the tools available for coaching are far more limited, and few leaders are given the time and resources to invest in them. So, with these limitations, how do you improve your coaching conversation game?

Before embarking on the journey of becoming a great leader/coach, it's important to reflect on your personal philosophy and approach to coaching conversations. If you skip this vital step, you may find yourself trying to hold coaching conversations with twenty-something millennials using an approach more suited to a baby-boomer, or vice-versa.

The origins of workplace coaching can be traced back to the post-WWII emergence of industrial psychology, and the development of the human potential movement (HPM) of the 1960s. Over the following 30 years, HPM established the framework on which modern coaching was built. From the mid-1980s through today, there have been several generations of approaches to workplace coaching:

- Performance and Productivity: The mid-1980s through the 1990s saw significant technology-driven productivity, and an associated focus on performance coaching. Total Quality Management, Business Process Reengineering, and forced employee rankings all contributed to a focus on 1-on-1 individual performance and productivity conversations in a "command-and-control" context.
- Goal Achievement: The mid-to-late 90s brought the dot-com boom, emerging Internet, Gen X workplace expectations, and the downfall of organizational hierarchy with the rise of knowledge workers. These set the stage for a shift in coaching emphasis away from individual performance and productivity improvement toward goal achievement. Along with these new approaches came a slew of proprietary "leader-as-coach" models and methods, replete with pseudoscience jargon (think, "neuroleadership"). Notably, most models retained the command-control approach of the prior generation, packed into 1-hour conversations.
- Continuous Performance Management: Nearly two decades into the 21st century, technology

> continues to accelerate changes in the way people work, and the Millennial generation is reshaping the relationship between employees and organizations. These mega-trends have inspired new approaches to coaching conversations that demonstrate agility, flexibility, and a genuine embrace of feedback.

As you reflect upon your coaching style and habits, ask yourself: are you stuck in the 1980s, welcoming the 21st century, or somewhere in between? Great coaching begins in the mirror. If you don't have a good grasp of your own values, a clear sense of where you find meaning and purpose in your work, a good sense your talents, strengths, and competencies, and an equally keen understanding of weaknesses and areas to improve, then how can you hope to credibly coach others—especially if they cross generations and cultures? At the heart of a coaching-conversation is the quality and authenticity of the relationship between the people having the discussion. Team coaching conversations occur between people who are striving together to achieve a goal. Before we turn to specific coaching strategies, it is important to understand the role your mindset plays in effective coaching.

I recall the feeling of satisfaction that came with my promotion to Director of Product Management in the early 1990s. I was charged with rapidly defining the next generation of products to drive the future growth of the company. The leadership coaching that I received was along the lines of "be good at what you do, constantly demonstrate your skills, and—if you want to be promoted—consistently perform better than others." It was a mindset that was all about me and what I could get from my team, not coaching them to be extraordinary. While somewhat embarrassing to admit now, at the time it seemed like sound advice as I was ambitious and eager to continue to climb the corporate ladder. And, for a while, it worked.

Less than a decade later, as my career progressed and as the pace of technological change and innovation began to accelerate, I witnessed the folly and painful consequences of an inwardly focused, narcissistic mindset among leaders. By the late 1990s, I was in a VP/GM role at Kodak responsible for the commercial imaging businesses. I vividly remember a conversation with Clay Christensen of Harvard Business School who was consulting with us at that time. The digital imaging units were struggling as technology and competitors were evolving rapidly around us. Yet, many team leaders were spending their time working to prove themselves in their current role and demonstrating that their skills (versus their team's capabilities and contribution) were better than others as they competed to move up in the organization. Looking back, Clay (very accurately) observed that if those leaders didn't change their focus to what they could do for their people and coach them to develop new skills and perform better versus the external environment, they would fail to inspire the energy and innovation they, and the company, would need to survive. Within a few years, people found themselves competing for deck chairs on a sinking ship.

If your mindset reflects what you want FOR your team versus what you want FROM your team, it will have a significant psychological impact on people. Supporting each team member's core psychological needs directly impacts individual and team development, performance, and satisfaction. Last, the more you exhibit a growth mindset in your conversations, the more responsive your people will be to your coaching.

With a growth mindset, you believe that people can develop their abilities, and get smarter and more talented by putting in time and effort. In contrast, if you assume abilities are relatively unchanging and believe that people either "have it or don't" when it comes to competencies and talents, then you are unlikely to get the best from your team. The rigidity of a closed mind is a road to obsolescence and irrelevance. You can't out-innovate the competition by following them. A growth mindset unlocks hidden value you otherwise would not have identified and developed. By learning to see the potential for extraordinary where others see only ordinary, you will dramatically increase the effectiveness of your coaching.

Your Team Coaching Strategy

In increasingly dynamic, complex business environments, helping people develop their strengths, build new competencies, and work collaboratively to deliver results has become a business imperative. Gallup's recently published research on *How Millennials Want to Work and Live* emphasized this fact with millennials asserting that they don't want to fix their weaknesses—they want to develop their strengths.

Your coaching strategy should be simple enough to implement given the reality of crazy-busy days, yet powerful enough to make a real difference to your team's performance. The challenge is ensuring that the good intentions associated with coaching don't result in the negative relationship experiences often reported by team members. While there are many coaching techniques and practices, at a broad level there are two dimensions of coaching strategy that you should always consider: the balance between facilitative and pressure-based coaching; and the balance between the coaching you do with your team members, versus your team members coaching (and being coached by) their peers.

Facilitative vs. Pressure-Based Coaching

The facilitative approach is feedback centric and frames coaching discussions around growth and performance. The emphasis of the discussion is on the alignment between team member and team objectives; guiding and assessing behaviors in accord with team norms; and closing relationship gaps. In contrast, pressure-based coaching discussions are framed by failure prevention and emphasize the consequences of failing to meet expectations. In pressure-based coaching, the manager provides direction by applying pressure to get results.

When asked which method they should employ, most people believe facilitative coaching is the superior choice. While that sounds like the 'right' answer, in reality, most managers tend to default to a pressure-based approach. Given the corporate world's obsession with quarterly results, this isn't surprising. In practice, both methods can deliver results in the short-term. The challenge is finding the right balance to deliver results in the long-term. Research (as well as my own experience) has shown that, over time, facilitative coaching produces greater commitment and improved performance, while disproportionate use of pressure-based coaching has a direct negative effect on team performance. Overuse of pressure-based coaching generates negative emotions and tensions that result in a deterioration of team commitment. Pressure-based coaching can be a useful tool, so long as you keep the duration short and use it sparingly. An imbalanced approach will result in the diminishment of team effectiveness, engagement, or both.

It is valuable to separate the creation of stretch objectives—or even big, audacious goals—from your coaching strategy in pursuit of those goals. Stretch goals are good. Set and communicated properly they focus and energize people to their best and beyond. Defaulting to a pressure-based approach in the day-to-day pursuit of those stretch goals, however, is a recipe for failure.

I've found that you can reach the optimal coaching-strategy balance with the following approach:

- Use facilitative coaching as your default.
- Selectively use pressure-based coaching to advance individual competencies and drive short-term results. For example, setting a deadline to boost someone's spreadsheet skill to complete the analysis of a new product proposal.

- Continuously seek feedback to ensure alignment between team member and team objectives; guiding and assessing behaviors in accord with team norms; and closing relationship gaps.

Leader or Peer Coaching?

The second dimension necessary for a successful coaching strategy is to find the best balance of who does the coaching. The 20th-century model was that the team leader is the coach; but there is another option that can be more effective, either alone or in conjunction with team leader coaching: peer coaching.

Recent research into the practices of consistently high-performing sports teams shows that the leadership qualities and actions demonstrated on the playing field by "athlete-leaders" have a significant impact on performance and satisfaction—the same holds true across all types of organizations. Shared leadership across the team can enhance performance.

Around ten years ago, I was working with my head of North American sales (we'll call him Mike) on improving his sales team's performance. Mike suggested that we needed to develop a more aggressive sales culture—including greater leverage in pay-for-performance—and engage in some intensive coaching. He also suggested that we remove a few of the weaker performers. If you led or worked in a sales organization in the 1980s and 1990s (as Mike had), those suggestions probably sound familiar, and to a large extent, the approach worked back then.

In the 21st-century, sales leaders face challenges far different from the 1980s and early 1990s. In a dynamic marketplace characterized by rapid product innovation, pricing information transparency, short product life-cycles, and intense competition, today's sales leaders must simultaneously convey a compelling vision; set clear, ambitious (but achievable) targets; hire, develop, and align diverse sales groups; and still deliver immediate results. So, I asked Mike to do some homework around current sales leadership practices, and after discussing our options, we chose a different path. Mike took a 4-step approach to facilitate shared leadership and peer coaching on his team:

Step 1: Identifying people's competency strengths and weaknesses. Mike sat with each person on the sales team and developed a profile of strengths, weaknesses, and needs. **NOTE:** You should use the Motivational Triangle to create a conversation that identifies skill development needs.

Step 2: Identifying peer coaches. Mike identified two team members who had the desire to coach, and competencies to share, that matched the needs of others on the team. Most importantly, they were respected by their peers.

Step 3: Setting clear expectations. Mike ensured that the people chosen to do the coaching, as well as the team members they coached, had a clear understanding of the objectives and key results.

Step 4: Measuring progress. Mike tracked the progress of individual competency development, as well as the overall team performance.

Step 5: Mike regularly sought feedback to ensure alignment and to identify any experience-expectation gaps between peer coaches and the others. He only stepped-in to coach the peer-coaches if the results showed signs of slipping.

Within three months, the underperforming sales reps had dramatically improved their numbers, as had the rest of the team. Within two quarters, the sales team was consistently exceeding their targets.

Peer coaching works, and it can be a game-changing approach to building and sustaining a highly-effective team. Recognize that the biggest challenge may be that your role, as you develop a team culture of shared leadership, must shift towards being a supporter versus a superior. You should find yourself spending more time supporting your peer-coaches than directing the team. Peer coaching also provides the added benefit of identifying and developing future leaders.

By calibrating the balance of facilitative and pressure-based coaching, as well as peer vs. leader coaching, you can develop a coaching strategy that consistently delivers a winning performance in the most complex, dynamic environments.

Up Your Coaching Conversation Game

The approach most golf coaches take to improving someone's game is to use a myriad of tools and techniques to fix multiple problems, combined with hours of range practice. Watching the pace and quality of play on any given weekend at your local golf course quickly highlights that those coaching efforts don't always translate to improved, on-course performance. Similarly, most advice about improving workplace coaching conversations begins with 'coaching models' that emphasize inputs, processes, and outputs, and lists of do's and don'ts, rules, roles, and responsibilities. The problem is, those approaches are often too complex to become a habit, and they address the symptoms rather than the problem.

Creating effective coaching conversations needn't be difficult (it's much easier than developing a consistent pitch shot!); however, it does need to be purposeful and practiced until it becomes a habit. The following three actions will take you a long way toward productive and pleasant coaching conversations:

First, make feedback an obsession. Most relationship breakdowns begin with a gap between what one or both people expect, versus their actual experience. Before you can coach, you need to understand where the discrepancies are in the key relationships.

Second, ensure psychological safety. Asking about expectations and related experiences is a safe approach to identifying relationship issues, as long as you are sensitive to some of the most common feelings that may undermine people's sense of psychological safety:

- A belief that mistakes may be held against them. Address this by establishing a clear norm that "mistakes equal learning," and when teammates fall short of each other's expectations, that they will close the gap quickly and without judgment.
- Sensing that being different can mean rejection. Again, this should be addressed by developing values that are used to guide and assess the team. Everyone must have an equal voice at the table.

- Believing that asking for help may be viewed as a weakness. Address this through your own actions —asking your people for help, and then encouraging others to do the same. Recognize that when this is missing on a team, so is trust.

Last, develop the habit of consistently healing experience-expectation gaps. Disparities between what people expect from their important relationships—team to leader, between teammates, and across groups—versus their actual experiences can fracture the heart of your team and diminish performance. It is because we are human that rifts develop between what people expect of each other and what they experience. We don't engage with one another via finely tuned algorithms, but through a messy mix of rational thought, emotions, preconceived ideas, and expectations—all viewed through the lens of our individual personalities and experiences. Closing gaps requires getting to their essence and understanding what the gap is, why is there a gap, and how to close the gap. To do that you should:

- Regularly gather feedback on team member expectations of each other, of you, and of the other teams that support them versus their actual experience.

- Openly discuss the feedback and acknowledge the existing issues, then prioritize them.
- Identify specific actions to close those differences.
- Track progress and repeat the cycle.

When to Coach

Events and experiences at work have their own rhythm that usually has little in common with the drumbeat of organizational review cycles. Historically, individual progress reviews (team level reviews being almost non-existent) were a once or twice a year process that focused on what had been accomplished, versus goals set at the beginning of the year—not what people learned, or what experience they gained. Moreover, these annual review processes were time-consuming, subject to multiple biases—especially recency bias, where the most recent activity and results have a disproportionate influence—and in my experience on both sides of the desk, highly unsatisfying.

Today, many organizations are moving to some form of continuous performance management with a focus on regular conversations, feedback, and recognition, which are distinctly separate from compensation. TRM is designed to be an integral part of the continuous-performance conversations. It provides both the context (regular coaching conversations) and content (rich feedback that addresses individual and team psychological needs) that bind together formal business objectives, the actions and behaviors that drive energy and engagement, and the rewards process.

Peter Drucker observed, "A manager's first role is the personal one. It's the relationship with people, the devel-

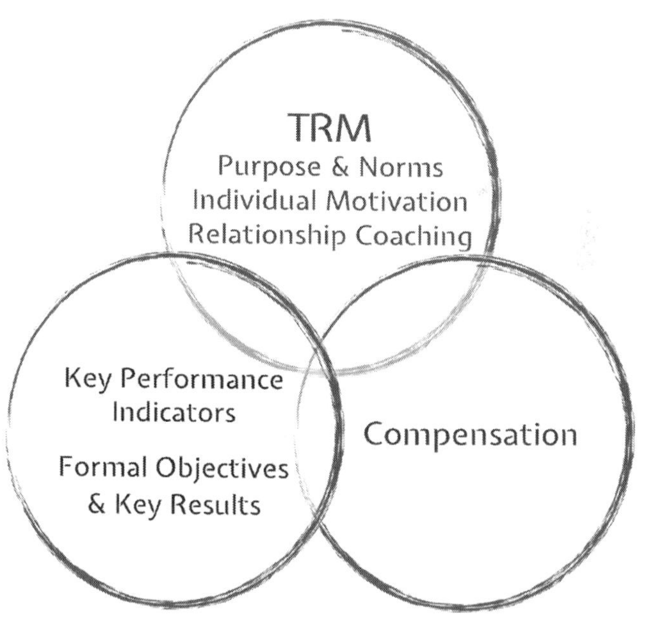

opment of mutual confidence... the creation of a community." If you want to craft an extraordinary team, focus on enhancing learning from people's day-to-day experiences. Pay attention to their growth over time, keep track of their experiences, and what competencies they developed. You can do that through the habit of regular conversations—both 1-on-1 and with your team:

- Weekly Individual Check-ins. Holding a weekly, short, one-on-one check-ins keep people energized. It is an opportunity to touch base on goals and progress, and to learn what you can do to support achieving them. The conversations should be biased towards asking questions versus giving direction and should support versus asking for a report. Be sure to discuss any existing experience-expectation issues and the progress on closing them.
- Monthly Team Reviews. These meetings should focus on your team's progress against existing goals, including closing gaps, ensuring alignment of goals, processes, and priorities, and reviewing the latest feedback for new gaps. Most importantly, these reviews should be action-oriented with clear ownership and follow-up on prior actions.

- Quarterly 1-on-1 Reviews. These once-per-quarter discussions around effort, performance, and career offer an opportunity to ensure clear alignment between each team member's role and objectives with that of the team and organization. It is also an opportunity to reinforce team culture, as well as the part each person plays in upholding those values—and, as always, allows you to address experience-expectation issues.

Team coaching is a collaborative process that builds strong relationships and group support. It encourages open communication among the individuals, and between you and your team members. Issues can be raised, and solutions explored in a way that encourages the creativity of all involved. Frequent coaching based upon regular feedback also keeps you aware of the frustrations or disconnects that can all too quickly lead to relationships deteriorating and people disengaging.

Most importantly, remember the basics of motivation—coaching is about taking something extrinsic (external feedback and support) and helping people internalize it as their own. People learn more and progress faster when they find purpose (and pleasure) in what they're doing.

So have fun as you coach!

Chapter Highlights

- Improving your coaching conversation game begins with reflecting on your personal philosophy of coaching conversations:
    - Develop a good grasp of your own values and have a clear sense of where you find meaning and purpose in your work
    - Have a good sense of your talents, strengths, and competencies
    - Have an equally keen understanding of your own weaknesses and areas to improve
- Your mindset plays a critical role in coaching. Focus on what you want FOR your team versus what you want FROM your team.
- A growth mindset reflects a belief that people can develop their abilities by putting in time and effort. Assuming people's abilities are unchanging is a fixed mindset that is unlikely to enable you to get the best from your team.
- Failing to seek honest input from your team can lead to reduced psychological safety, loss of trust, the deterioration of critical relationships, and ultimately disengagement.

- Exceptional leaders and their teams don't treat feedback as an activity to be added to already busy workdays; seeking feedback and proactively responding to it is a habit that forms an integral part of a leader's role.
- Despite the critical role of teams, few leaders measure the most critical predictors of effectiveness over time—the health of the relationships on and across teams.
- Measuring relationship strength and expectations versus experience gaps, and identifying who's working on closing them, keeps people aligned and fosters trust.
- Relationship metrics are like radar for your team. The relationship metrics that you should be using are:
  - Experience-expectation gaps
  - Team relationship strength
- There are two basic coaching strategies that you will use—a balance between facilitative and pressure-based coaching, and between the coaching you do versus peer coaching.

- Creating effective coaching conversations should be purposeful and practiced until it becomes a habit. Three actions will take you a long way toward productive and pleasant coaching conversations:
    - Make feedback an obsession.
    - Ensure psychological safety.
    - Develop the habit of consistently healing experience-expectation gaps.
- Organizations are moving to continuous performance management with a focus on regular conversations, feedback, and recognition, and are distinctly separate from compensation. TRM is designed to be an integral part of those continuous performance conversations.
- At the heart of team-coaching is the quality of the relationship between people. Do it right, and you will create a vibrant, diverse group where talented people are committed to one another and passionate about their work.

Thoughts & Notes

Thoughts & Notes

Team Coaching

1. What is your personal philosophy and mindset about coaching conversations?
2. How do you currently seek feedback from your team?
3. What are the state of the relationships on your team (and how do you know?)
4. How will you integrate TRM into your continuous performance conversations?

Thoughts & Notes

Thoughts & Notes

Team Coaching

What is your strategy to balance:

1. Facilitative vs. Pressure Based
2. Peer vs Leader Coaching

Thoughts & Notes

Crafting an Extraordinary Team

"If I have seen further, it is by standing on the shoulders of giants."

–Isaac Newton

During my doctoral research, I discovered that there are as many definitions of leadership as there are people attempting to define it. For much of the 20th century, those definitions focused on leader traits and behaviors that produced hero leaders and the organizational hierarchies they oversaw. That model is quickly being relegated to the history books. The essence of today's team leader role is one of crafting, not commanding. You must be willing to set the bar high in terms of both performance and behavior and serve as a model for meeting those standards. In addition, it is important that you develop relationships of reciprocity on and across teams that enable people to work effectively across borders and boundaries, understanding the fluid and complex nature of your role and teamwork in a global, networked world as you guide your team to becoming extraordinary.

Crafting an extraordinary team means establishing a relationship architecture that becomes self-sustaining. The three actions required to establish that architecture includes laying a foundation that helps people bring their whole self to work; understanding what motivates each of your team members—knowing what gets them out of bed energized every day; and developing the team relationship coaching habits that foster trust and commitment. In doing so, you not only position your team for

A Word on Leaders and Legacy

As I write this concluding chapter, I'm going to violate my "no clichés" rule just this once because there is more than just a modicum of truth in the statement that, "people don't quit their job, they quit their boss." People may quit because the manager is truly toxic, or perhaps he or she is well intended—and even successful in terms of performance versus goals—but fails to create an environment in which people can thrive both professionally and personally. In either case, the leader has failed to understand the human dimensions that are the lifeblood of the best teams and the stuff of which lasting leadership legacies are made.

Over the course of my career, I've watched many managers destroy the goodwill and well-being of the people on their team for the sake of achieving a short-term goal. Often, these efforts are focused on delivering results that were committed to without the buy-in from the team. Even when everyone 'drinks the Kool-Aid' and makes the sacrifices necessary to achieve the goal handed to them, I can't recall a single instance when a leader was remembered for "that great second quarter in 2017", or "delivering that new product on schedule back in '15". People don't remember the financial or business results of the last quarter, let alone a few years

success, but you also create a legacy for yourself that lasts long after you've moved on to greater responsibilities and new career heights.

Summary: Your Three Actions

There are two questions you should frequently ask yourself: "Why does my team want to be led by me?" and, "Am I creating the best conditions for my team to thrive in terms of both performance and well-being?" The first question can be quite humbling. The second holds the answer to the first.

Where you will struggle to find the answer is in the thousands of books and articles published every year on the topic of 'leadership'. From *How to Lead Yourself, How to Thrive, How to Get People to Help You,* and *How to Stay Relevant and Reinvent Yourself* to *Professionalizing Leadership* and *Leadership That Matters* (to name a tiny fraction of title excerpts from recent books), the advice is endless—and complex.

Paraphrasing William of Ockham, my experience has been that in almost any endeavor, simpler solutions are more likely to be implemented—and more successful in their implementation. Throughout this book, I've laid the groundwork for the three actions that get to the very

back. Legacies are built on the strength of human connections. This is especially true for first-level leaders. You have a tremendous effect on the well-being of the people on your team. The ultimate compliment you can get is when the best people from your early teams want to join you again, and everyone remembers you for the positive influence you had on their personal and professional development and career.

essence of what leads to exceptional team performance. If you execute them well and develop them into habits, you will answer those two vital questions and find yourself, and your team, on the road to extraordinary.

Action One: Find Purpose & Instill Healthy Norms

Establish a clear, compelling team purpose and develop the habit of using norms to guide and assess your team.

Most importantly, your team's norms should be shared by everyone, and they should reflect the core values necessary to build and sustain effective, robust relationships. At a minimum, these should include psychological safety, and developing a strong sense of mutual expectations, mutual voice and influence, and mutual trust.

Our Team Norms
Eliminate bias
Honesty and candor
Everyone has equal voice
Everyone owns the customer

Thoughts & Notes

Describe your team's purpose and norms

Action Two: Inspire Individual Motivation

Develop the habit of inspiring individual motivation through regular conversations around each team member's Motivational Triangle.

Focus on the connection between the purpose people find in their work, and the team's purpose and goals. You want to create a world to which people want to belong—where their individual identities (their values and talents) are affirmed, and where they are inspired to contribute to something larger than themselves by helping them to develop the means (competencies) and giving them the autonomy to pursue their purpose.

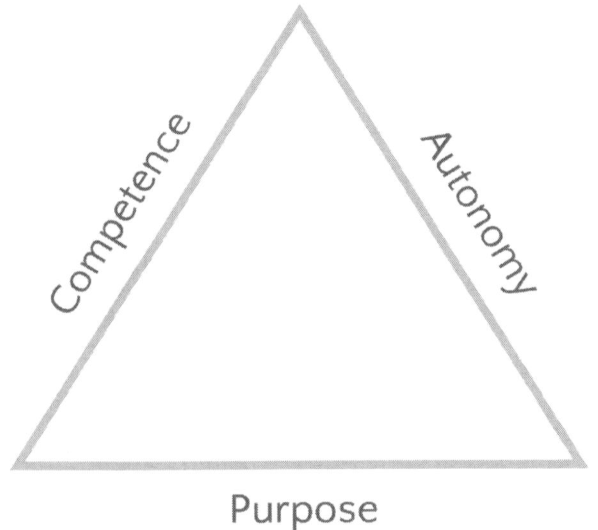

Thoughts & Notes

Team Member Motivational Triangles

Purpose:

Competence:

Autonomy:

Action Three: Team Relationship Coaching

Develop the habit of conducting team coaching conversations based upon identifying, measuring, and tracking relationship strength and closing experience-expectation gaps.

Relationship coaching is what sustains the energy on a team, and builds strong, trusting relationships that lay the foundation for extraordinary performance. Great coaching begins in the mirror, recognizes that individuals want and need different things if their potential is to be realized, and balances those needs with the needs of the team and organization.

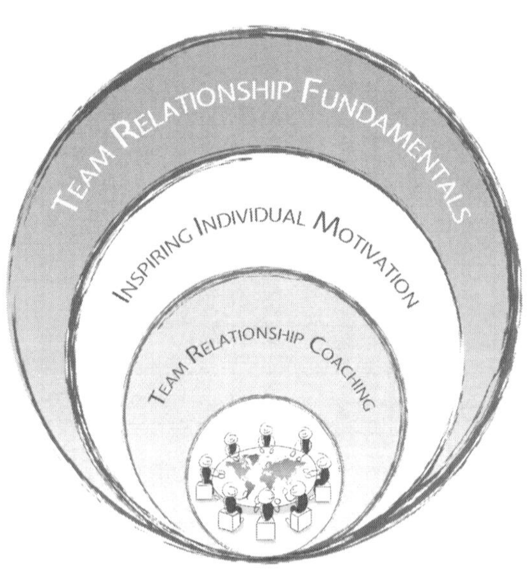

Thoughts & Notes

What is your coaching conversation strategy?

Reflections

"We are what we repeatedly do.
Excellence, then, is not an act, but a habit."

~Aristotle, 384–322 BCE

Over the course of my five-year 'walkabout' in the shoes of today's team leaders, and my research into what it takes to craft exceptional 21st-century teams, I saw how trends from the use of global virtual teams and millennials taking on leadership roles, to changes in performance management processes and new communications technologies, are transforming businesses. Strategy and structure have become more dynamic, with hierarchies flattening and vastly more work being done by teams. Yet, too often, I still saw and experienced command-and-control management practices in a world of digital natives and fluid networks. The result was diminished energy and engagement and wasted potential for both organizations and people.

Thriving in the 21st century demands that organizations reshape themselves around teams and networks of teams, and that they evolve mindsets from "leadership belonging to a single person or specific role", to "leadership as a collaborative process that is shared across networks of people". At the forefront of this evolution are the people now transitioning from individual contributor to team leader and people manager. This transition is one of the most significant turning points for both businesses and people, because it increasingly involves millennial leaders.

Gallup reinforced the vital importance of those leadership transitions in their research on *How Millennials Want to Work and Live*. The results show that millennials and prior generations have many similarities; but, where there are differences, the differences are dramatic. Millennials have strong biases towards specific dimensions of the employee experience that are fundamentally altering the nature of work. Gallup uncovered six attitudes and associated expectations that employers must deliver against if they want to attract and retain the best young talent:

1. Millennials don't just work for a paycheck—they want a purpose.
2. Millennials are not pursuing job satisfaction—they are pursuing development.
3. Millennials don't want bosses—they want coaches.
4. Millennials don't want annual reviews—they want ongoing conversations.
5. Millennials don't want to fix their weaknesses—they want to develop their strengths.
6. Millennials don't want a job—they want a good job.

The expectations of over 80 million millennials, along with the generations before them who are reassessing their approach to work, emphasize the vital importance of mastering the art of team relationship management. TRM should be a focal point for every 21st-century team leader, whether you are just starting your leadership journey, or are a more experienced manager wanting to stay relevant in the face of rapid change in the way we work. Mastering TRM means:

- Being the catalyst that ignites a steadfast determination to excel.
- Embracing the idea that success depends less on your skills or brilliance and more on your humility and ability to inspire the best in people.
- And ultimately, developing the few key habits that lead to an extraordinary team—laying a foundation of enduring trust, encouraging behaviors that inspire, and coaching that keeps relationships strong.

TRM offers the opportunity to ensure that your team will thrive. Your resolve to instill the habits of TRM in your team plays a critical role in determining whether your organization ends up as a historical footnote, languishes in mediocrity, or is on the road to enduring greatness. In the end, team leadership in the 21st century is about making people more effective while striving to ensure their well-being. And because we're human, with all our idiosyncrasies and complexities, there will never be "one best way." But paraphrasing the words of Thomas Edison, there will always be a better way. Our role as a leader is to be unrelenting in our quest to find it.

At the risk of being criticized for promoting commercial products and services, I've included information on TRM software tools for team leaders, and The TRM workshop in the following Appendices. I included them because, at the time of publication, there were no other dedicated tools available to support team leaders in developing and instilling the habits of TRM. Both the Xmetryx TRM software and the TRM Workshop emerged out of my research, and were co-designed with team leaders and their teams from around the world.

Appendix A: TRM Coaching Tools

XMETRYX TRM™

If you want extraordinary you must get relationships. We developed Xmetryx TRM tools to help leaders accelerate the effectiveness of team relationship coaching. The tools provide an innovative, cost-effective (less than buying a cappuccino for each team member every month) means of measuring, visualizing, and tracking relationship strength. Using Xmetryx TRM helps you develop the strong, trusting relationships that are the foundation of every exceptional team, dramatically reducing risk and significantly improving performance.

Xmetryx TRM tools are designed to enhance team relationship coaching by identifying what's energizing and motivating people, as well as measuring relationship gaps on and across teams before they lead to deteriorating performance and disengagement. By capturing people's experience versus their expectation, and the reason for any gap, you get immediate insights into the most important issues that are supporting or interfering with team effectiveness and well-being.

Xmetryx TRM measures expectations (the circumstances that form a baseline psychological contract) and experiences (the contextual and psychological factors that determine need satisfaction and meaningfulness), then predicts the strength and state of key relationships on vibrant, visual maps. You can use that feedback to create transformational coaching conversations with your team, and then use Experience Tracking to monitor the progress of your efforts to close gaps.

The design of Xmetryx TRM assumes that, in the context of the organization, team, and specific goals, employees can best identify what is most important to their well-being and effectiveness. The software reflects a modern foundation of research and practice at the intersection of behavioral science, neuroscience, and graphic design:

- Behavioral science demonstrates the power of focusing on understanding a person's experience versus their expectation relative to a goal and across the relationships that are important to achieving that goal. Developing a feedback survey from the "inside-out".
- Neuroscience research shows the critical importance of capturing both affective (emotions) and cognitive (thinking) feedback. Despite these insights, most survey methods used today—which were developed in the early 20th century—don't provide an effective means of capturing both aspects. The neuroscience bridge to 21st-century surveys is facial expressions, as they are

one of the most important cues in both affective and cognitive communication. Extensive research into human-computer interaction demonstrates that emoticons (or emoji) are an effective way to make up for many of the cues absent in text-based communications. Well-designed interactive emoji mimic facial expressions and encourage the expression of feelings. These should form the core of an "inside-out" employee survey.

- Interactive survey-design combines the experience-expectation questions that uncover the key issues interfering with people's performance and happiness, with emoji facial expression animation that enables greater emotional expressiveness and makes the survey itself more engaging. The result is a rich picture of a team's experience, energy, and engagement while eliminating survey fatigue and encouraging frequent use.

The Xmetryx TRM Feedback Tool™

The Xmetryx TRM Feedback Tool (patent pending) has only three questions and takes about three minutes to complete. You can use the Feedback Tool to gather insights from your teams—local or virtual—on a regular basis without cutting into already overloaded work days. It's fast, engaging, and delivers powerful insights based upon both affective (feeling) and cognitive (thinking) inputs. People can provide feedback on any device—desktop, tablet, or mobile. Within Xmetryx TRM, the question format is designed to do three things:

- Get at the heart of each employee's experience by focusing on what is most important to them in key relationships with direct managers, coworkers, and other teams.
- Maintain consistency in questioning for comparison over time.
- Prevent the introduction of bias, to ensure that you're getting accurate data on which you can act.

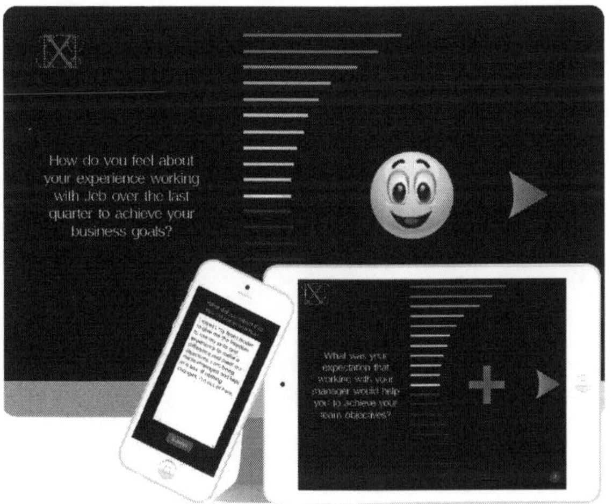

The Feedback Tool provides flexibility while maintaining quality and consistency. Keep in mind that, while it is not a general survey tool, with Xmetryx TRM you can customize the subject, type of goal, and the time frame that was given to accomplish the goal. The key to robust feedback is not the number of questions you ask, but what you ask. The Xmetryx TRM questions have been carefully constructed to evoke valuable, candid feedback without bias.

The Xmetryx Experience Map™

It is our experiences versus our expectations (in the context of critical relationships) that affect the course of our relationships: engaging or disengaging; developing or deteriorating. The Xmetryx TRM Experience Map plots each team member's experience relative to their expectations (as captured by the Xmetryx TRM Feedback Tool). This provides you with a comprehensive picture of any experience-expectation gaps, along with candid feedback that will help guide you in closing those gaps.

The Experience Map is divided into four quadrants, each which indicates the direction the relationship is headed (counterclockwise from top-right): Engaging, Deteriorating, Disengaging, and Developing). Each area also represents the strength of the relationship: strong, degrading, or strengthening.

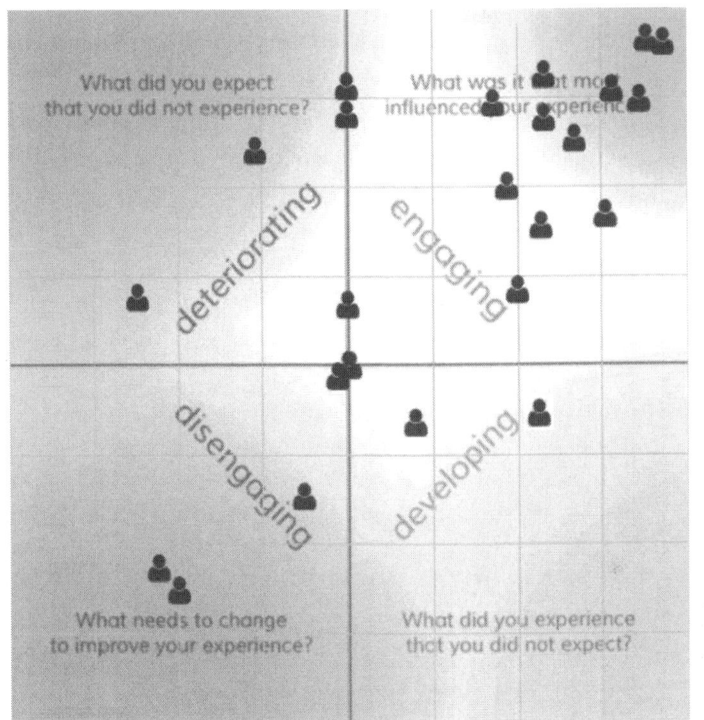

EXAMPLE EXPERIENCE MAP

The Engaging Quadrant

This is your target quadrant. It indicates team members who have consistently good experiences with high expectations. Team members in this quadrant are likely to have a shared sense of purpose, clear goals, and feel that there are healthy relationships among the team, with coworkers, and with the team leader. You are building trust, loyalty, and confidence that will fuel ongoing team energy, engagement, and performance.

Relationship Strength

People in the top 1/2 of this quadrant fall into the "Healthy Relationship" category (see the section on Relationship Strength Score below). These people have a strong positive effect on the rest of the team, helping to bring the group up as a whole.

People in the lower 1/2 of this quadrant, while not dissatisfied, are not strongly positive and do not have a notable impact on the rest of the team; therefore, they fall into the "Strengthening Relationship" category.

Actions to Take

You are on the path to crafting an extraordinary team. Continue to reinforce the fundamentals of highly-effective teams, ensuring clarity of team purpose and healthy norms. Driving your Relationship Strength Score towards 100 requires:

- Laying and then reinforcing a foundation that helps people bring their whole self to work
- Understanding what motivates each of your team members—knowing what gets them out of bed energized every day
- And, developing the team relationship coaching habits that foster trust and commitment

The Deteriorating Quadrant

This is a transition quadrant and presents team members with negative experiences and high expectations. These employees, at one time, had good experiences, which built their high expectations, but their experiences have recently turned negative. If you don't address these issues, they will lead to mistrust, uncertainty, and a transition to disengagement.

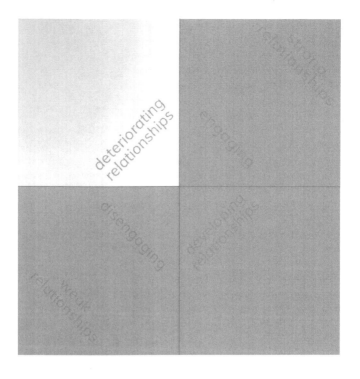

Relationship Strength

When people fall into this quadrant, it is a red flag that their dissatisfaction can start to affect others on the team. Consequently, this group falls into the "Toxic Relationship" category.

Actions to Take

- Review your relationship fundamentals to identify any weaknesses
- Focus on clarity in team purpose and goals, as well as team values (especially psychological safety)
- At a team level, review and discuss the Experience Map, asking for team input on needed changes to improve overall experiences
- At an individual level, get clarity on each team member's Motivational Triangle and their expectations versus experience across key relationships. Develop an action plan with owners and timing to close gaps

The Disengaging Quadrant

This is your crisis quadrant and characterizes those who have negative experiences and low expectations. A person in this quadrant is likely to be toxic—drawing energy away from others on the team, negatively impacting productivity and performance, and potentially driving turnover.

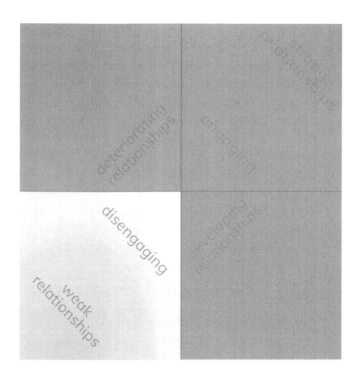

Relationship Strength

Due to the severity of the impact people in this quadrant have on the team's ability to perform as well as the overall spirit of the individuals, they fall into the "Degrading Relationship" category.

Actions to Take

If most of the team members fall into this quadrant, then there is likely an issue with the team leader. If the number of people in this quadrant is small:

- Start with 1-on-1 Motivational Triangle discussions to determine who has significant gaps
- In the context of that conversation, identify and prioritize the experiences which will raise expectations
- If you do not see rapid improvement, consider moving the individual(s) to a different role or team that might offer a better fit

The Developing Quadrant

This is a transition quadrant which is characterized by employees with Low to Moderate Expectations and Positive Experiences. These people are encouraged by their recent experiences but do not yet have strong trust, loyalty, or confidence, which moderates their expectations.

Relationship Strength

People in this group are still finding their feet, so they do not yet fall into the strong relationship category; but, with your help, they are on their way! At this point, they fall into the "Strengthening Relationship" category.

Actions to Take

Continue to focus on team fundamentals—in particular, clarity of purpose and team values that encourage participation—as well as the key drivers of motivation at work: individual purpose, competence/confidence building through training and knowledge, and increasing autonomy as competencies develop.

In addition, ensure that you quickly close any disparities in their experiences versus what they're expecting. Your goal is to consistently exceed expectations until they are solidly in the Engaging Quadrant.

We are what we repeatedly do. Developing the one habit of continually closing experience-expectation gaps across pivotal relationships—as you build an energized, engaged, and highly-effective team—requires discipline and perseverance.

Tracking Progress

Xmetryx Experience Maps can be combined to track progress as you close these experience-expectation gaps. The ability to set notifications and automated reminders —as well as view the Xmetryx Relationship Strength Score Trend, where you can see the change in the strength of your team's relationship over time—helps you visualize your progress. It also helps you establish habits that will move your team solidly into the engaging quadrant.

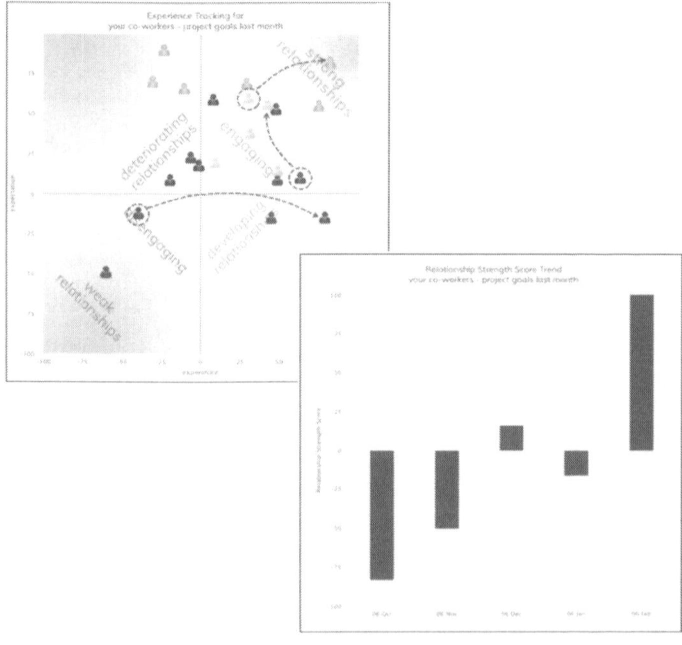

Xmetryx TRM Relationship Strength Score™

The Relationship Strength Score measures the strength of people's critical relationships based upon their reported experience versus their expectation. Relationships are broken down into three categories, based upon the results from the Xmetryx TRM Feedback Tool:

Strong Relationships—those with highly-positive experiences and high expectations—have a positive impact on the well-being of other team members, and the performance of the team as a whole.

Degrading Relationships—those with negative experiences, regardless of their expectations—have a strong negative effect on the team's productivity and can cause negativity, mistrust, and uncertainty to spread among the team members.

Strengthening Relationships—those whose experiences are positive, but still have low/negative expectations; or whose experiences are only mildly positive regardless of their expectations—don't have a substantial influence on other people's experiences, either positive or negative.

Xmetryx TRM calculates the Relationship Strength Score by subtracting the percentage of Degrading Relationships from the Strong Relationships (the Strengthening Relationships do not impact the score). This highlights the overall strength of the relationships in your group. It ranges from -100 (all Degrading Relationships) to 100 (all Strong Relationships).

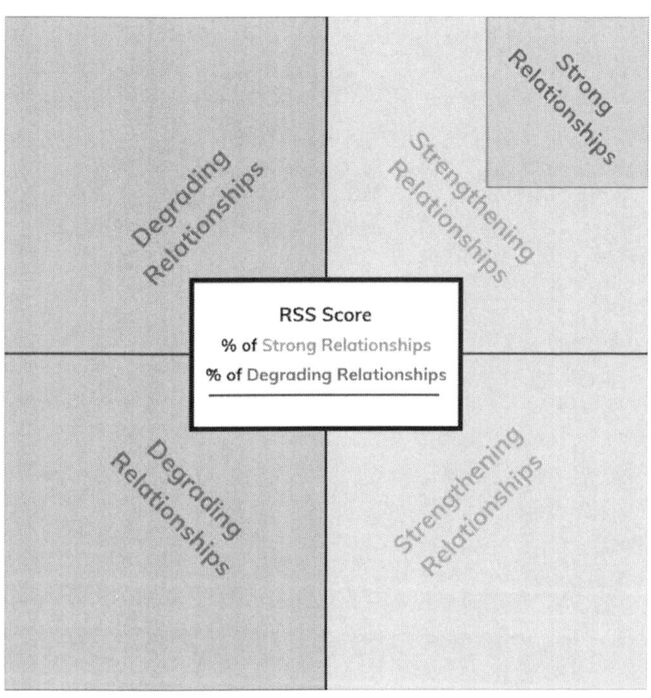

Continuous Feedback

Gathering insights regularly—weekly, monthly, and quarterly—is the first step to maintaining healthy relationships and requires ongoing, active participation from your team. It is essential to review the Xmetryx TRM Feedback Tool and methodology with your team, emphasizing the importance of their candid feedback, and reassuring them that their responses are completely anonymous.

Relationship coaching is what sustains the energy on a team, and builds strong, trusting relationships that lay the foundation for extraordinary performance. Xmetryx TRM gives you powerful feedback, measurement, and tracking tools that will act as both a mirror and radar for you and your team. The tools enable you to recognize individual wants and needs, and balance those needs with the needs of the team and organization, closing gaps as they arise.

Appendix B: The TRM Workshop

The TRM Workshop was co-designed with team leaders from around the world. It is based on modern team science and the practices of exceptional teams. The TRM Workshop is your fast-track to placing groups of team leaders on the path to crafting extraordinary teams.

The Workshop Highlights

TRM isn't your typical leader-development workshop. You won't get slides full of pop-psychology clichés or blind-folded tinker-toy exercises. You will get a day of experiential learning that gives you coaching and tools to craft an extraordinary team. By the end of the day you will:

- Understand the power and importance of team purpose and norms
- Master the Motivational Triangle and learn to apply that knowledge in 1-on-1 coaching conversations
- Discover the fundamentals of Team Relationship Coaching and creating effective team coaching conversations
- Learn to use TRM (Team Relationship Management) tools to measure team development and coach your team

- Embrace the three actions that quickly improve team performance, engagement, and well-being.

Why TRM? Because team leaders who master the art of team relationship management:

- Ignite a steadfast determination in their team to excel
- Embrace the idea that success depends less on skills or brilliance and more on humility and ability to inspire the best in people
- Lay a foundation of enduring trust, encourage behaviors that inspire, and coach to keep relationships strong

Beyond the Workshop

Innovative new ideas and practices can be challenging to implement, especially when every day feels like you're changing tires on a moving car. We're going to break that cycle by going together Beyond the Workshop. Beyond the Workshop gives every workshop attendee:

- **Resources:** a pdf of The Workshop Concepts, Notes, Actions, & Checklists to help you start implementing the TRM concepts immediately
- **Team Assessment:** a complimentary Xmetryx TRM Baseline Assessment of their your team
- **Personalized Recommendations:** Dr. Hurley will guide the implementation of your deployment of Xmetryx TRM tools

With *Beyond the Workshop* you will turn the ideas and skills you've learned into actions that lead to an exceptional team. In addition to the complimentary support, Dr. Hurley can be booked for leadership coaching sessions. Contact us to discuss your needs:

workshops@xmetryx.com

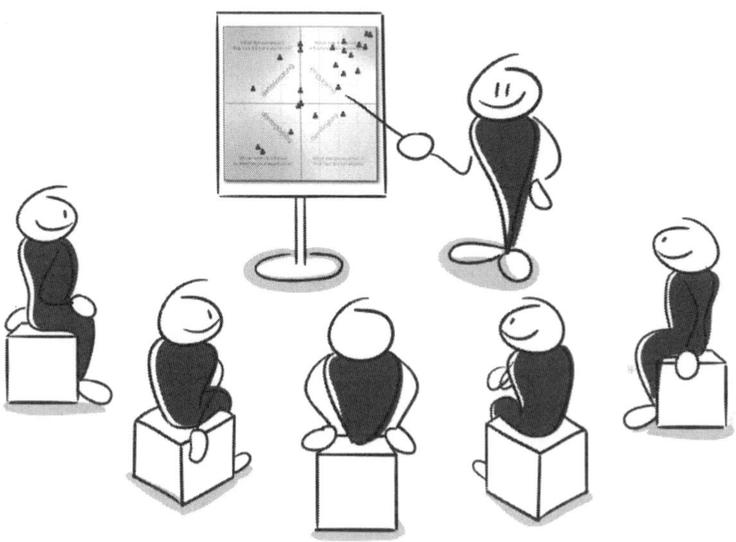

Appendix C: Foundations of TRM

I learned a lot about myself when I turned 16 and my dad first put me on the sales floor. Somewhat shy by nature, I found my confidence to talk with adults about complex and expensive products by learning everything I could about what we offered as well as items offered by our competitors. I found that only when I understood the underlying technology, and believed deeply in the value of a product, was I very effective at selling it. It's an aspect of myself that has never changed. Later in life, as I became a voracious consumer of books and articles on leadership, I was often disappointed by author's who were 'selling' a point of view that was neither built upon a deep understanding of the topic nor broad-based, validated research. A trend which seems to have only accelerated in recent years.

The principle underlying research foundation of TRM, and more specifically The Motivational Triangle, is based upon one of the most broadly-tested and validated contemporary theories of human motivation—Self-Determination Theory. If you're someone that likes to return to "first principles," and gain a sense of the giants upon whose shoulders an idea was built (to paraphrase Newton), this appendix is for you (includes in-text citations).

Self Determination Theory

From the turn of the 19th century through the decade following World War II, Western experimental and applied psychologists studied behavioral and psychodynamic motivational drive theories. With the advent of cognitive motivation theories, scholars lost interest in behavioral and psychodynamic motivational drive constructs (Deci & Ryan, 1985). During the latter part of the 20th century and the early part of the 21st century, researchers showed interest in evolved and acquired needs, and intrinsic motivation, and revived scholarship on motivational theories (Ryan, 2012). During this revival, Deci and Ryan (1985) articulated a macro-theory of motivation: self-determination theory (SDT). Deci and Ryan (2000) differentiated SDT from other motivational constructs by distinguishing types and quality of motivation versus singular, additive concepts that focused on the total amount of motivation. In subsequent studies, researchers confirmed the validity of the core idea that motivational type or quality predicts performance, well-being, and other outcomes (Deci & Ryan, 2008).

Two central concepts of SDT are human need–satisfaction and need-frustration. Scholars examine the satisfaction-frustration continuum in the context of autonomous and controlled work motivation (Vandercammen, Hofmans, & Theuns, 2014). According to SDT, people are, by nature, intellectually and experientially active, and driven by the desire to find purpose and realize possibilities (Dysvik et al., 2013). SDT scholars assume that people are proactive in their desire to optimize their life situation (Van Yperen, Wörtler, & De Jonge, 2016). Autonomous motivation includes a blend of intrinsic motivators, plus extrinsic motivators that have sufficient meaning to become intrinsic in their expression. According to SDT, people internalize extrinsic motivation across a continuum in varying degrees, with a correlated effect on perceived autonomy (Sisley & Smollan, 2012). The SDT continuum (Figure 1) depicts the spectrum from amotivation to intrinsic motivation.

Within SDT, satisfaction of three basic, universal psychological needs, autonomy, competence, and relatedness, is related to intrinsic motivation (Dysvik et al., 2013). Deci and Ryan (1985) elaborated on these three basic needs within two SDT sub-theories they termed cognitive evaluation theory (CET) and organismic integration theory (OIT). Autonomy refers to people's sense of control over their own behavior and its outcomes. Researchers found that autonomous motivation indicates and predicts positive affect (Gillet, Vallerand, Lafrenière, & Bureau, 2012). Competence refers to people's need to acquire and demonstrate capabilities and capacities.

Because they need to perceive themselves as competent, people engage in actions and behaviors that bolster their sense of competence (Fay & Sonnentag, 2012). Relatedness (Purpose in the Motivational Triangle tool) refers to people's need to belong to a broader community, as well as to believe that they contribute to that community and the individuals within it (Dysvik et al., 2013).

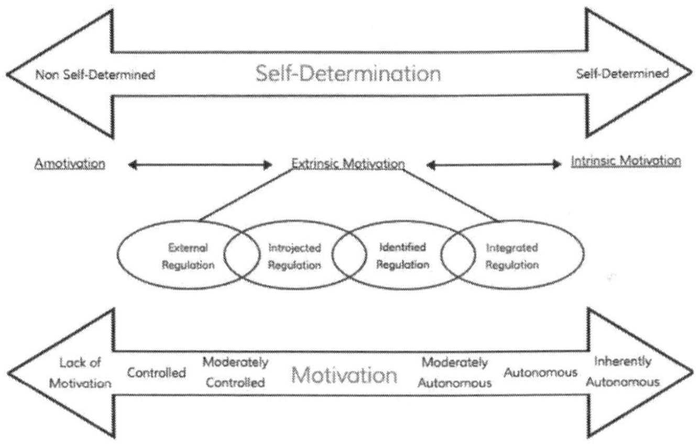

Figure 1. The spectrum of motivation types and subtypes within SDT. Regulatory subtypes are: external, introjected, identified, and integrated. Amotivation describes a state without action or intent. Intrinsic motivation describes autonomous, self-actualized energy and behavior. The four sub-

Types of extrinsic motivation represent states that range from low autonomy and internal motivation (external regulation), to highly autonomous and fully absorbed behavior, though still outside of intrinsically motivated action (integrated regulation). Adapted with permission from "Self-Determination Theory and The Facilitation of Intrinsic Motivation, Social Development, and Well-Being," by R. M. Ryan and E. L. Deci, 2000, American Psychologist, 55, p. 72. Copyright 2000 by the American Psychological Association.

Deci and Ryan (1985) proposed that the need for autonomy, competence, and relatedness are universal and operate across cultures. Testing this assertion, Church et al. (2013) conducted an eight-culture study covering the United States, Australia, Mexico, Venezuela, Japan, China, Malaysia, and the Philippines. They found that, while people's perceptions of need-satisfaction show variations across cultures, the core SDT needs are cross-culturally consistent and important to need-fulfillment. Earlier, van Beek et al. (2012) found, in their research in China, that autonomy, competence, and relatedness were core motivational drivers. Roche and Haar (2013) conducted research in New Zealand across 250 organizations to test the full SDT metamodel, and found a significant relationship among the elements of

SDT related to the facilitator variables of aspirations, motivations, and mindfulness. In testing the full SDT metamodel, the researchers also identified a significant relationship between the elements of SDT and the core psychological needs of autonomy, competence, and relatedness (Roche & Haar, 2013).

Self-Determination Theory at Work

As the nature of work within an organizational environment becomes more complex, so does the leader's need to understand and influence the forces that encourage work-related motivation (Dysvik et al., 2013). Within SDT, the relationship between employees and their organizational environment predicts individual behavior and motivation. Van Beek et al. (2012) found a relationship between the type of motivation, the basic needs for autonomy, competence, and relatedness, and employee behavior.

Figure 1 depicts this relationship within SDT across a spectrum, which ranges from amotivation to autonomous, self-determined motivation (Gagné & Deci, 2005). Researchers have given the SDT construct of motivation quality the most attention as they searched for the determinants of autonomous, self-determined work motivation (Gillet, Gagné, Sauvagère, & Fouquereau, 2013). As

Gagné and Deci (2005) envisioned, the outcome of the employee's range of behavioral regulation reflects the quality of motivation. For example, in a Swiss study of 201 insurance industry employees, Guntert (2014) found a significant relationship between positive work outcomes and both extrinsic identified regulation and intrinsic motivation. More specifically, Guntert demonstrated that the CET and OIT sub-theories of SDT were distinct, yet complementary, cross-culturally relevant predictors of positive work outcomes. Those work outcomes included job satisfaction, turnover intent, and organizational citizenship behavior.

Within the context of SDT, Gagné and Deci (2005) defined autonomously motivated employees as people who performed because they found purpose and meaning in their work. Conversely, the researchers viewed employees who acted primarily because of external (extrinsic) demands as controlled and lacking autonomous motivation. Fernet, Austin, and Vallerand (2012) conducted a longitudinal study with 586 participants in which they examined both autonomous and controlled motivation in relation to work motivation. The authors concluded that organizational support of autonomous motivation promoted employee work motivation in the form of higher levels of commitment and lower exhaustion from work. Supporting those results, researchers conducted multiple studies showing that employees who experience high-quality, autonomous motivation exhibit positive performance, increased satisfaction, and higher levels of commitment (Trépanier, Fernet, & Austin, 2013).

SDT is an approach to understanding what motivates people to seek purpose and take action based upon the proposition that people have universal psychological needs. In the organizational and work context, researchers use SDT to explain the relationship between employee needs and work motivation (Deci & Ryan, 2000). While people's perceptions of need-satisfaction vary across cultures, the concepts of needs in SDT are cross-culturally consistent and important to need-satisfaction (Church et al., 2013). In their research exploring the integration of transformational leadership, basic psychological needs as defined in SDT, and work engagement, Kovjanic et al. (2013) provided additional empirical support for Deci and Ryan's (2000) assertion of the relationship between employee needs and work motivation. Kovjanic et al. demonstrated the link between the fulfillment of the need for autonomy, competence, and relatedness, and employee engagement and performance.

The contents of Appendix C are an excerpt from "Engagement Strategies for Catalyzing IT Sales Team Performance in Asia". Adapted with permission from the author.

References

Church, A. T., Katigbak, M. S., Locke, K. D., Zhang, H., Shen, J., de Jesús Vargas-Flores, J., … Ching, C. M. (2013). Need satisfaction and well-being: Testing self-determination theory in eight cultures. *Journal of Cross-Cultural Psychology*, 44, 507-534. doi:10.1177/0022022112466590

Deci, E. L., & Ryan, R. M. (1985). *Intrinsic motivation and self-determination in human behavior*. New York, NY: Plenum.

Deci, E. L., & Ryan, R. M. (2012). Motivation, personality, and development within embedded social contexts: An overview of self-determination theory. In R. M. Ryan (Ed.), *The Oxford handbook of human motivation* (pp. 85-107). New York, NY: Oxford University Press.

DeCooman, R., Stynen, D., Van den Broeck, A., Sels, L., & De Witte, H. (2013). How job characteristics relate to need satisfaction and autonomous motivation: Implications for work effort. *Journal of Applied Social Psychology*, 43, 1342-1352. doi:10.1111-/jasp.12143

Dysvik, A., Kuvaas, B., & Gagné, M. (2013). An investigation of the unique, synergistic and balanced relationships between basic psychological needs and intrinsic motivation. *Journal of Applied Social Psychology*, 43, 1050-1064. doi:10.1111/jasp.12068

Fay, D., & Sonnentag, S. (2012). Within-person fluctuations of proactive behavior: How affect and experienced competence regulate work behavior. *Human Performance*, 25, 72-93. doi:10.1080/08959285.2011.631647

Fernet, C., Austin, S., & Vallerand, R. J. (2012). The effects of work motivation on employee exhaustion and commitment: An extension of the JD-R model. *Work & Stress*, 26, 213-229. doi:10.1080/02678373.2012.713202

Gagné, M., & Deci, E. L. (2005). Self-determination theory and work motivation. *Journal of Organizational Behavior*, 26, 331-362. doi:10.1002/job.322

Gillet, N., Gagné, M., Sauvagère, S., & Fouquereau, E. (2013). The role of supervisor autonomy support, organizational support, and autonomous and controlled motivation in predicting employees' satisfaction and turnover intentions. *European Journal of Work and Organizational Psychology*, 22, 450-460. doi:10.1080/1359432X.2012.665228

Gillet, N., Vallerand, R. J., Lafrenière, M. K., & Bureau, J. S. (2012). The mediating role of positive and negative affect in the situational motivation-performance relationship. *Motivation and Emotion*, 37, 465-479. doi:10.1007/s11031-012-9314-5

Guntert, S. (2014). The impact of work design, autonomy support, and strategy on employee outcomes: A differentiated perspective on self-determination at work. *Motivation and Emotion*, 39, 99-103. doi:10.1007/s11031-014-9412-7

Kovjanic, S., Schuh, S. C., & Jonas, K. (2013). Transformational leadership and performance: An experimental investigation of the mediating effects of basic needs satisfaction and work engagement. *Journal of Occupational & Organizational Psychology*, 86, 543-555. doi:10.1111/joop.12022

Roche, M., & Haar, J. M. (2013). A metamodel approach towards self-determination theory: A study of New Zealand managers' organisational citizenship behaviours. *The International Journal of Human Resource Management*, 24, 3397-3417. doi:10.1080/09585192.2013.770779

Ryan, R. M. (2012). Motivation and the organization of human behavior: Three reasons for the reemergence of a field. In R. M. Ryan (Ed.), *The Oxford handbook of human motivation* (pp. 3-10). New York, NY: Oxford University Press.

Ryan, R. M., & Deci, E. L. (2000). Self-determination theory and the facilitation of intrinsic motivation, social development, and well-being. *American Psychologist*, 55, 68-78.

Sisley, R., & Smollan, R. (2012). Emotional labour and self-determination theory: A continuum of extrinsic and intrinsic causes of emotional expression and control. *New Zealand Journal of Employment Relations*, 38(2), 41-57. Retrieved from http://www.nzjournal.org/

Trépanier, S. G., Fernet, C., & Austin, S. (2013). The moderating role of autonomous motivation in the job demands-strain relation: A two sample study. *Motivation and Emotion*, 37, 93-105. doi:10.1007/s11031-012-9290-9 van Beek, I., Hu, Q., Schaufeli, W. B., Taris, T. W., & Schreurs, B. H. (2012). For fun, love, or money: What drives workaholic, engaged, and burned-out employees at work? *Applied Psychology: An International Review*, 61, 30-55. doi:10.1111/j.1464-0597.2011.00454.x

Van Yperen, N. W., Wörtler, B., & De Jonge, K. M. (2016). Workers' intrinsic work motivation when job demands are high: The role of need for autonomy and perceived opportunity for blended working. *Computers in Human Behavior*, 60, 179-184. doi:10.1016/j.chb.2016.02.068

Vandercammen, L., Hofmans, J., & Theuns, P. (2014). The mediating role of affect in the relationship between need satisfaction and autonomous motivation. *Journal of Occupational & Organizational Psychology*, 87, 62-79. doi:10.1111/joop.12032

Additional Reading & Select References

Aldunate, N., & González-Ibáñez, R. (2016). An Integrated Review of Emoticons in Computer-Mediated Communication. *Frontiers in Psychology*, 7, 2061. http://doi.org/10.3389/fpsyg.2016.02061

Alismail, S., & Zhang, H. (2018). The Use of Emoji in Electronic User Experience Questionnaire: An Exploratory Case Study.

Allen, J. A., Reiter-Palmon, R., Crowe, J., & Scott, C. (2018). Debriefs: Team learning from doing in context. *American Psychologist*, 73, 504-516.

Battistelli, A., Galletta, M., Portoghese, I., & Vandenberghe, C. (2013). Mindsets of commitment and motivation: Interrelationships and contribution to work outcomes. *The Journal of Psychology*, 147, 17–48. doi:10.1080/00223980.2012.668146

Beck, K., Grenning, J., Martin, R. C., Beedle, M., Highsmith, J., Mellor, S., van Bennekum, A., Hunt, A., Schwaber, K., Cockburn, A., Jeffries, R., Sutherland, J., Cunningham, W., Kern, J., Thomas, D., Fowler, M., Marick, B. (2001). Manifesto for Agile Software Development. Agile Alliance.

Beer, M., Finnström, M., Schrader, D. (October, 2016). Why leadership training fails - and what to do about it. *Harvard Business Review*, 10, 50–57. https://hbr.org/2016/10/why-leadership¬training-fails-and-what-to-do-about-it

Bell, S. T., Brown, S. G., Colaneri, A., & Outland, N. (2018). Team composition and the ABCs of teamwork. *American Psychologist*, 73, 349–362.

Bellott, F. K., & Tutor, F. D. (1990). "A Challenge to the Conventional Wisdom of Herzberg and Maslow Theories." Paper presented at the Nineteenth Annual Meeting of the Mid-South Educational Research Association. New Orleans, LA.

Bennis, W. (1999). *The Leadership Advantage: Leader to Leader*. Hoboken, N.J.: Jossey-Bass.

Blackwell Landon, L., Slack, K. J., & Barrett, J. D. (2018). Teamwork and collaboration in long-duration space missions: Going to extremes. *American Psychologist*, 73, 563–575.

Bruce, K. (2006). Henry S. Dennison, Elton Mayo, and Human Relations historiography. *Management & Organizational History*. 1:2, 177—199. doi: 10.1177/1744935906064095.

Burke, C. S., Stagl, K. C., Klein, C., Goodwin, G. E., Salas, E., &Halpin, S. (2006). What types of leader behaviors are functional in teams?: A meta-analysis. *Leadership Quarterly*, 288-307.

Chen, G., Kirkman, B. L., Kanfer, R., Allen, D., & Rosen, B. 2007. A multilevel study of leadership, empowerment, and performance in teams. *Journal of Applied Psychology*, 92, 331-346.

Deci, E. L., & Ryan, R. M. (1985). *Intrinsic Motivation and Self-determination in Human Behavior*. New York, NY: Plenum

Deci, E. L., & Ryan, R. M. (2012). Motivation, personality, and development within embedded social contexts: An overview of self-determination theory. In R. M. Ryan (Ed.), T*he Oxford Handbook of Human Motivation*, (pp. 85–107). New York, NY: Oxford University Press.

Doerr, J. (2018). *Measure What Matters: How Google, Bono, and the Gates Foundation Rock the World with OKRs*. New York: Penguin Random-House.

Dunlap, J., Bose, D., Lowenthal, P. R., York, C. S., Atkinson, M., & Murtagh, J. (in press). What sunshine is to flowers: A literature review on the use of emoticons to support online learning. To appear in *Emotions, Design, Learning and Technology*. Elsevier.

Gagné, M., & Deci, E. L. (2005). Self-determination theory and work motivation. *Journal of Organizational Behavior*, 26, 331–362. doi:10.1002/job.322

Hurley, J.S. (2017). Engagement Strategies for Catalyzing IT Sales Team Performance in Asia. Retrieved from https://scholarworks.waldenu.edu/dissertations/3784/

Hurley, J. (2017). *The ONE Habit: The Ultimate Guide to Increasing Engagement and Building Highly-Effective Teams*. Scottsdale: Xmetryx Press. ISBN: 9780692900994. https://www.xmetryx.com

Judd, S., O'Rourke, E., and Grant, A. (2018). Employee Surveys Are Still One of the Best Ways to Measure Engagement. *Harvard Business Review*. https://hbr.org/2018/03/employee-surveys-are-still-one-of-the-best-ways-to-measure-engagement

Kahn, W. A. (1990). Psychological conditions of personal engagement and disengagement at work. *Academy of Management Journal*, 33, 692–724. doi:10.2307/256287

Kaplan, M., Dollar, B., Melian, V., Van Durme, Y., & Wong, J. (2016). Human capital trends 2016 survey. Oakland, CA: *Deloitte University Press*. Retrieved from https://www2.deloitte.com/insights/us/en/focus/human-capital-trends.html

Kouzes, L., Posner, B. (2017). *The Leadership Challenge: How to Make Extraordinary Things Happen in Organizations.* 6th Ed. Hoboken: Jossey-Bass Publishers. ISBN: 978-1119278962

Lacerenza, C. N., Marlow, S. L., Tannenbaum, S. I., & Salas, E. (2018). Team development interventions: Evidence-based approaches for improving teamwork. *American Psychologist*, 73(4), 517-531. doi:10.1037/amp0000295

Maslow, A.H. (1943). A theory of human motivation. *Psychological Review*. 50 (4): 370–96. CiteSeerX 10.1.1.334.7586. doi:10.1037/h0054346

McChrystal, S., Tantum, C., Silverman, D., Fussell, C. (2015). *Team of Teams: New Rules of Engagement for a Complex World*. New York: Penguin Publishing Group. ISBN 978-1591847489)

Moran, A. (2014). *Agile Risk Management*. Springer Verlag. ISBN 978-3319050072.

Morrel-Samuels, P. (2002). Getting the Truth into Workplace Surveys. *Harvard Business Review*. https://hbr.org/2002/02/getting-the-truth-into-workplace-surveys

Ryan, R. M., & Deci, E. L. (2000). Self-determination theory and the facilitation of intrinsic motivation, social development, and well-being. *American Psychologist*, 55, 68–78. doi:10.1037/0003¬066X.55.1.68

Schaufeli, W. B. (2013). What is engagement? In C. Truss, K. Alfes, R. Delbridge, A. Shantz, and E.C. Soane (Eds.), *Employee Engagement in Theory and Practice*, (pp. 1–38) London: Routledge.

Truss, C., Shantz, A., Soane, E., Alfes, K., & Delbridge, R. (2013). Employee engagement, organisational performance and individual well-being: Exploring the evidence, developing the theory. International *Journal of Human Resource Management*, 24, 2657– 2669. doi:10.1080/09585192.2013.798921

Wahba, M. A., & Bridwell, L. G. (1976). Maslow reconsidered: A review of research on the need hierarchy theory. *Organizational Behavior & Human Performance*, 15(2), 212-240. http://dx.doi.org/10.1016/0030-5073(76)90038-6

Glossary

Agile Manifesto

In 2001, seventeen software developers met at the Snowbird ski resort in the Wasatch mountains of Utah to discuss faster, lighter software development methods. Together they published the Manifesto for Agile Software Development. The four values described in the Manifesto were:

- Individuals and interactions over processes and tools
- Working software over comprehensive documentation
- Customer collaboration over contract negotiation
- Responding to change over following a plan

The Manifesto for Agile Software Development is based on twelve principles that support breaking product development work into small increments known as sprints that minimize the amount of up-front planning and design. Each sprint involves a cross-functional team that is tasked with demonstrating a working product, or feature of a product, at the end of the sprint, with the goal of minimizing overall risk and allowing the product to adapt to changes quickly.

Beck, K., Grenning, J., Martin, R. C., Beedle, M., Highsmith, J., Mellor, S., van Bennekum, A., Hunt, A., Schwaber, K., Cockburn, A., Jeffries, R., Sutherland, J., Cunningham, W., Kern, J., Thomas, D., Fowler, M., Marick, B. (2001). Manifesto for Agile Software Development. Agile Alliance.

Moran, A. (2014). Agile Risk Management. Springer Verlag. ISBN 978-3319050072.

Autonomy

Identified within Self-determination Theory (SDT) as one of three universal psychological needs that drives human motivation, Autonomy is the need to have control over one's own role and priorities.

See Self-Determination Theory

Competence

One of three universal psychological needs identified within SDT that drives human motivation, Competence is the need to develop and demonstrate one's capabilities and capacities.

See Self-Determination Theory

Engagement Theory

At the intersection of employee well-being and performance lies the concept of engagement. Over the past 25 years, engagement has become a ubiquitous construct within business. In his seminal research on personal engagement and disengagement at work, Kahn (1990) introduced the engagement framework which describes how work experience and work context inform personal engagement and task performance.

Kahn, W. A. (1990). Psychological conditions of personal engagement and disengagement at work. Academy of Management Journal, 33, 692–724. doi:10.2307/256287

Expectancy Disconfirmation Theory

As noted by R. L. Oliver (1977 and 1980), expectancy disconfirmation theory (alternatively expectation disconfirmation theory, expectation confirmation theory, ECT) is a cognitive theory which seeks to explain the impact of expectations, and confirmation / disconfirmation of (experience with) those expectations.

Oliver R. L, (1977), "Effect of Expectation and Disconfirmation on Postexposure Product Evaluations – an Alternative Interpretation," *Journal of Applied Psychology*, 62(4), p. 480.

Oliver R. L, (1980). A Cognitive Model of the Antecedents and Consequences of Satisfaction Decisions, *Journal of Marketing Research*, 17(4), p. 460.

Expectations

Expectations can be defined as an individual's belief about the experience he or she will have in a given scenario. Expectations can be the result of past experience with similar situations, or knowledge about other peoples' experiences with similar situations.

Olson, J. C., & Dover, P. (1976). Effects of Expectation Creation and Disconfirmation on Belief Elements of Cognitive Structure, in B. B. Anderson, ed., *Advances in Consumer Research, Volume III*, Chicago: Association for Consumer Research, 168–75.

LaTour, S. A., Peat, N. C. (1979). Conceptual and Methodological Issues in Consumer Satisfaction Research, in *Advances in Consumer Research,* (Vol. 6), ed. William L. Wilkie, Ann Arbor: Association for Consumer Research, 431–440.

Human Relations Movement

The human relations movement began as a collection of ideas that were highlighted in the 1930's with sociologist George Elton Mayo's experiments known as the Hawthorne studies, which examined the effects of social relations, motivation, and employee satisfaction on factory productivity. Mayo's studies demonstrated that when employers focus on employee needs and psychological makeup productivity increases. Important factors included:

- The power of natural groups.
- The need for reciprocal communication.
- The development of high-quality leadership.

The human relations movement represented a turning point in the development of management practices. The introduction of insights from the behavioral sciences initially helped managers to understand how to increase productivity and set the stage for research into the importance and effect of every individual in a company – and how they can meet their individual needs while benefiting their organization.

Bruce, K. (2006). Henry S. Dennison, Elton Mayo, and Human Relations historiography, Management & Organizational History, 1:2, 177–199. doi: 10.1177/1744935906064095.

Job Design

Job design is the process of putting together a range of tasks, duties, and responsibilities to create a composite for individuals to undertake in their work and to regard as their own.

Torrington et al., 2011. Human Resource Management. 8th Edition. Harlow: Pearson.

Key Relationships

Key work relationships are those relationships that have a high degree of impact on goal achievement, career advancement, and role satisfaction. They are characterized by a high degree of both emotional (affective) and cognitive engagement. Consider not just the job itself, but also the way the team member is intended to interact with those around them. The primary key relationships, as mentioned in this guide, are:

- The relationship between a team member and his or her team leader.
- The relationship between a team member and another person on the same team.
- The relationship between a team member and people on other teams).

Maslow's Hierarchy of Needs

Abraham Maslow published his hierarchy of needs theory in his 1943 paper "A Theory of Human Motivation" in Psychological Review." Maslow hypothesized that people experience needs in generally the same hierarchical pattern, and that pattern requires substantially satisfying the current need before fulfilling the next need.

Maslow's hierarchy of needs is often shown as a pyramid with the survival need at the bottom and the self-actualization need at the top. In the work context, applying Maslow's hierarchy implied that as an employee advances through an organization, there are greater opportunities to satisfy needs higher on Maslow's pyramid.

Key criticisms of Maslow's Hierarchy include questioning whether human needs are hierarchical; that the theory doesn't account for changing needs; and that it is primarily a Western model versus universal. Empirical research has not substantiated the concept of a human need hierarchy. Wahba and Bridwell (1976) showed that there was little evidence for Maslow's ranking of these needs and even less evidence that these needs are in a hierarchical order. Despite the conceptual weakness, Maslow's work signaled a shift in psychological research and practice from abnormal behavior and development to the development of healthy individuals.

Maslow, A.H. (1943). "A theory of human motivation". Psychological Review. 50 (4): 370–96. CiteSeerX 10.1.1.334.7586. doi:10.1037/h0054346

Psychological Contract Theory

A psychological contract, a concept developed in contemporary research by organizational scholar Denise Rousseau, represents the mutual beliefs, perceptions, and informal obligations between an employer and an employee. It sets the dynamics for the relationship and defines the detailed practicality of the work to be done.

Rousseau, D. M. (1989). Psychological and implied contracts in organizations. Employee Responsibilities and Rights Journal, 2: 121–139. https://www.wikiwand.com/en/Psychological_contract

Purpose

One of three universal psychological needs that drives human motivation, Purpose is the sense of belonging and believing that one's work makes a difference.

See Self-Determination Theory

Role Content

Designed to enable people to find their work meaningful, and to help them feel that the work they do matters and makes a difference. Role content should:

- Foster a sense of responsibility and allow people to see the link between the work they do and the end results of their work.
- Allow people to use their current skills and develop new ones.

- See how their work contributes to a 'whole piece' of work.
- Have a sense of autonomy.
- Receive regular and constructive feedback.

Role Context

Role context comprises the reality of the organizational culture, the team norms, everyday work processes, the nature of key relationships and dependencies, as well as key measures of success. It also frames the conditions under which work is performed and the demands such work imposes on employees. Good role context should clearly identify:

- Reporting relationships
- Supervision received
- Judgment, authority
- Personal contacts (key relationships)
- Physical and mental demands

Self-Determination Theory

Self-Determination Theory (SDT) is a theory of motivation. It is concerned with supporting our natural (intrinsic) tendencies to behave in effective and healthy ways. SDT has been researched and practiced by a network of researchers around the world. www.selfdeterminationtheory.org

Deci, E. L., & Ryan, R. M. (1985). Intrinsic Motivation and Self-determination in Human Behavior. New York, NY: Plenum

Team Norms

The traditions, behavioral standards, and unwritten rules of a group. For example:

- The methods team members use interact and communicate with each other.
- The methods team members use to communicate with members of other teams.
- The methods team members use to take responsibility and accountability for accomplishing their group goals.

Team Relationship Management

An approach to develop a team's key relationships (intra-team, team-to-leader, and across teams) to enhance effectiveness and individual well-being. Using feedback and data analysis about key team member relationships, TRM enables team leaders to understand and influence the critical team processes and behaviors that lead to strong, trusting relationships. Those relationships are the foundation of exceptional team performance, increased engagement, and improved satisfaction.

The TRM concept originated at the intersection of research into human motivation, employee engagement, and team effectiveness. The foundation underlying TRM is broad and deep, and is built upon the four pillars of: Self-Determination Theory; Engagement Theory; Expectancy Disconfirmation Theory; and Psychological Contract Theory.

At the core of TRM is the practice of understanding people's experiences versus their expectations. The power of TRM comes from identifying and measuring experience-expectation gaps and tracking relationship strength. Decades of research shows that disparities between people's experiences and expectations can harm relationships and diminish performance. Consistently addressing and closing relationship gaps builds the trust that spurs engagement, performance, and satisfaction.

Theory X and Theory Y

In the 1950s, Douglas McGregor (1906-1964), a psychologist and professor at MIT, criticized both the classical and human relations schools as "out of touch" with the realities of the workplace, and as representing a negative view of human nature. McGregor presented his Theory X and Theory Y as two sets of assumptions about human nature and human behavior that were more relevant to work and management at that time. He laid out his ideas in his 1957 article "The Human Side of Enterprise" and the 1960 book of the same name.

Theory X represents a view of human nature that assumes individuals generally dislike work and require close supervision to do their jobs. Theory Y denotes a view of human nature that assumes individuals are generally hard-working and able to assume responsibility and exercise self-control in their jobs. McGregor believed that Theory Y assumptions, such as decentralization of decision-making authority and participative management would lead to more effective management.

In the mid to later part of the 20th century McGregor's conceptualization of Theory X and Theory Y were often used as the basis for discussions of management style, employee involvement, and worker motivation. Empirical evidence concerning the validity of McGregor's theory, however, has been mixed. Some researchers suggest that organizations implementing Theory Y tended to revert back to Theory X in tough economic times. Critics contend that, rather than concern for employees, Theory Y in practice focusing on measures of productivity rather than measures of employee well-being. Employees are seduced into working harder for the same pay.

McGregor's work on Theory X and Theory Y has had a significant impact on management thought. Today, Theory X and Theory Y are often studied as a prelude to developing greater understanding of more recent management concepts and motivational theories such as the job-characteristics model self-determination theory.

INDEX

A

B

C

D

E

F

G

H

K

L

M

S

T

U

V

W

X

Thoughts & Notes

"The dullest pencil is better than the sharpest memory."

~Mark Twain

Thoughts & Notes

Thoughts & Notes

Thoughts & Notes

Thoughts & Notes

Thoughts & Notes

Thoughts & Notes

Thoughts & Notes

Thoughts & Notes

Thoughts & Notes

Thoughts & Notes

About the Author

"Leadership legacies are built on the strength of human connections."
~Jeb S. Hurley

Dr. Jeb Hurley, DBA has deep expertise in team science and team leader development. His passion is inspiring leaders to craft extraordinary teams - teams that deliver exceptional performance while providing experiences that enhance the quality of the lives of everyone on them. Jeb's career journey began on new product innovation teams in Europe and Asia. Those formative experiences led to GM / VP and CEO roles at companies ranging from Fortune 500 to VC backed start-ups and co-founding three software start-ups.

Jeb's research and work with teams highlighted that solving complex problems with innovative solutions requires the collaboration of the best minds, yet too often trust is low, and people are disengaged resulting in a spiral towards team mediocrity or worse. At the heart of that struggle is a failure to develop strong, trusting relationships that are the foundation of team performance and individual well-being. Those insights led to Jeb co-founding Xmetryx, a Team Relationship Management software company.

Jeb regularly speaks and writes about team leadership and improving employee well-being. His TRM Workshop is based upon his groundbreaking research into human motivation, engagement, and team performance. Jeb is the author of *Team Relationship Management: The Art of Crafting Extraordinary Teams* and *The ONE Habit: The Ultimate Guide to Increasing Engagement & Building Highly-Effective Teams*. He has published over 50 articles on team leadership and is a Featured Contributor for BIZCATALYST360°.